EVERGREEN

Designed to help you grow from nothing, to a life forever green

——————— Jake Mires ———————

For more information, you may email evergreenbook@yahoo.com

- First edition -

Dedicated to my wife.

Without you I would have nothing, I would be nothing.

You have inspired me to build a life for you I could have never imagined before.

The joy you have brought me has surpassed any financial or physical form. You have given my life

purpose and meaning and I am forever in debt to you for it.

I would like to thank you. Thank you for staying by my side, through the uncertainty and stress, the

18 hour work days and constant phone calls. Thank you for listing to my ideas at 2 a.m. and thank

you for the relentless support you have given me throughout our journey to success.

Through hard work and perseverance we have grown immensely and will continue to grow to build

a life that will allow us to be our best selves without financial stress or strain.

The best is yet to come.

"Real estate cannot be lost or stolen, nor can it be carried away. Purchased with common sense, paid in full, and managed with reasonable care, it is about the safest investment in the world."

-Franklin D. Roosevelt, 32nd U.S. President

"If you don't own a home, buy one. If you own a home, buy another one. If you own two homes, buy a third and lend your relatives the money to buy a home"

-John Paulson, investor and multi-billionaire

Contents

EVERGREEN

Evergreen (ev-er-green) noun. *A plant that retains green leaves throughout the year.*

My goal in writing this book is to give you tools you can use to create financial freedom through real estate investing (don't get discouraged, real estate investing isn't as hard as it sounds). Living an evergreen (financially free) lifestyle simply means to always have money flowing to you. No matter where you are or what you're doing, your wallet is always green. Yes, just like an evergreen tree you will eventually shed some leaves (lose some money), but you will always have new fresh leaves sprouting right around the corner. Year after year you will keep adding branches and leaves growing your net worth and cash flow. To live like this it takes patience, deep roots and a strong foundation.

While on your journey to this evergreen lifestyle, don't let money control you. You will never be happy if you only search for dollars. You will constantly be chasing that next dollar until you're dead. The true meaning of success is not to be rich, but to be financially free and fulfilled.

Financial freedom can mean many different things to many different people. For me, financial freedom is about living life on my terms. Doing what I want, when I want, how I want. If I want something, I buy it. If I want to go somewhere, I go. Imagine living life without the burden of time or financial stress. Not worrying about buying your plane tickets on the third Wednesday of the month at 5:03 p.m. because this is supposed to be the cheapest time to buy flights. Life is too short to worry about these things. Take the steps today, to live the rest of your life evergreen.

There is a common problem in our modern society. We either have too much time and not enough money, or too much money and not enough time to enjoy it. What's the use of being a millionaire or billionaire if you can't enjoy what you've worked so hard for? In the beginning of our lives all we care about is money, later in life all we care about is time. Living an evergreen lifestyle will help you balance the two. You will have a constant flow of money coming in and free time to truly enjoy it.

I believe in destiny. You picked this book up for a reason, you're the type of person who wants to get ahead and create a life many people only dream of. For that, I commend you. There aren't many people like you. Most people would rather watch TV or sit on their phone all day, but you're taking the steps to build something bigger, gain the power to make big moves and live life like it was meant to be lived. Congratulations on taking the first step to your bright future.

HOW I GOT STARTED

I didn't grow up in a traditional household. Nobody in my family worked a 9-5 job to make ends meet. My grandfather owned a shoe repair shop to provide for his family. He has always told me to work for myself, he said there's no other way. He always did well, as a young kid we always went on vacation with my grandparents. They had a nice RV and would take me and my cousins to the beach regularly. I never really questioned it. They went wherever they wanted, whenever they wanted. I just thought they were cool grandparents. I wouldn't realize the power of financial freedom until much later.

My dad is a professional musician and my mom was a stay at home mother. My dad did everything he could to provide for our family. He had many different business ventures. When I started high school, my parents opened a music store. I thought it was the coolest thing. He could pick his own name, he could choose what he wanted to sell and what hours he worked. Nobody could tell him what to do. Upon opening this new business, he would work from 6am to around 9pm (sometimes later) every single day. Not every once in a while, every single day. I always wondered what would makes someone work this hard. Going to school for six hours a day killed me enough. I couldn't fathom working 15 or 16 hour days, seven days a week.

After a few years passed I started to realize why he worked so hard. It was all for our family. He worked 15 hours every day so that our family could have whatever we wanted, and we did. We weren't rich by any means, but the life he created allowed us to have the freedom to do what we wanted without a heavy burden of time or money. You don't need millions of dollars to have fun and live in abundance. If you are smart with your money and use it the right way, it won't take much to create a very full life for you and your family.

After many long talks with him I came to realize how important it was to work for yourself. Owning your own business and working for yourself means unlimited earning potential. If you make $15 per hour, that's it, no matter how hard you work, you will make $15 per hour. Being someone who is self employed, if you work harder than anyone else, your income can be limitless. You aren't bound by any constraints.

In order to get everything you want in life you have to work these 15 hour days. You have to work harder than the next person. If living in abundance was easy, everyone would be doing it. Realizing that building a life like my father gave me wouldn't be easy. I had to get smart and get ahead. In attempt to get ahead, I took my senior year of high school at our community college. I was able to finish high school and also take some college classes at the same time. I thought this would be the easiest way to get ahead. Instead of learning and actually getting ahead, I spent most of my time folding envelopes in detention for being late or just not showing up to class.

I don't get along with school very well. I've always looked at it as a waste of time. In my opinion, the only thing school does is give you validation that you can work hard and finish things. I didn't buy it. Instead of going to college to get a degree, I set out to learn as much as I possibly could. In doing this I took every business class my community college had to offer. While taking these business classes I always found myself daydreaming. I didn't want to work the same job until I was 65, that seemed boring. I wanted more.

During my time at school I made it my mission to conjure up the best way to beat the rat race. I spent every day drawing out plans, running numbers and researching professions. I concluded, nobody gets ahead in life by working a 9-5 job and retiring. You couldn't live in abundance this way unless you were a doctor, lawyer, hedge fund manager or another high earning profession. These are all careers that cost a lot of time and money up front. The most simple way to boost your income and start earning enough to invest, save and reinvest is to get into one of these careers that have unlimited earning potential like a loan officer, real estate agent, or simply owning your own business. Even though you are working for yourself, you still have to take risks and work hard to get ahead, simple as that. There are no get rich quick shortcuts. That popular saying "You have to risk it, to get the biscuit" is too real. After researching successful people and listening to success story after success story, it became overwhelming that real estate is the best way to plan for your future, be financially free and create wealth. It has been said that real estate is responsible for creating 90% of the worlds millionaires and billionaires.

After learning a little bit about real estate and how powerful it was. I didn't jump right in. I always kept it in the back of my mind. I knew it was something I wanted to do, but didn't know when or how. I tried other things to create passive income first.

My grandfather finally retired and shut his shoe repair shop down. At the age of 17, me, my brother and our friend moved into this space to live and also used it as a music venue for local bands to play. After hosting a few shows and charging $5-$10 per person at the door, we began paying our bills with this money. It became really popular. About 2 months in, we had bands from New York, Florida and even Canada coming through California wanting to play at our venue.

Living there, we each worked normal jobs at local coffee shops. We would work from 5am to about 2pm, and start setting up for a show after that. We wouldn't go to sleep until well after 2am. I can remember a time when we went on tour in our own band and had a show in San Jose, CA before having to come back home. This is about a four hour drive from our hometown. We got done playing and left the city around midnight to start our four hour drive home. By the time we got home we had to shower and head right into work. We did anything to keep the dream alive.

We eventually got tired of dealing with unorganized bands and drunk people we didn't know thrashing our house. So me, my brother, my friend and my now wife packed everything we had and moved to Portland, OR for a change of scenery. This was an adventure all in it's own.

After living broke in Portland for a while I got an amazing opportunity to work at the Nike world headquarters in Beaverton, OR. I thought I had my life made. I was working on the weekdays and surfing on the weekends. Life was good until I realized like every other job I had before this, I didn't like anyone else telling me what to do. I wanted to do things my way. After about two years living in Portland I came to the realization that I needed to make bigger moves if I wanted to create the life I always dreamed of.

I finally decided to make the move on real estate that I had always wanted. I signed up online to get my real estate license in California. I woke up at 3am every morning for 8 months and studied for three hours before I had to go to work at 6am.

After finishing my courses and passing my final exam, I moved back to my home town in California to become a real estate agent and real estate investor. Nearly 6 months later I achieved one of my life long goals, to buy my own home. Purchasing my first real estate deal at 22 years old really made me realize it wasn't as hard as some people make it seem.

Although nothing comes easy, you have to make strategic moves and gain the knowledge before you can be successful in anything. Real estate will bring you everything you've ever dreamed of. In this book I will share my knowledge and strategies with you that you can implement today to create financial freedom whether you're already an investor and want to take your investing to the next level, or you're brand new and want to start.

Making the choice to start investing is the single most important decision you will make in your investment journey. When asked what regrets investors have later in life, they almost always say that they wish they would have started investing sooner. Although any age is better than not investing, the sooner you start investing the more your investments will compound and reward you. Investing is for the patient. Don't get discouraged if things aren't coming together as soon as you would like.

Once you make your first investment, I guarantee you will want to do another. I have talked to many other real estate investors and the majority have said that the first deal is the hardest. It's hard to break the ice and buy your first property. There are very few people who own only one investment property. After you acquire your first investment property and see the paycheck coming in every month growing your net worth without you doing anything, you will be glad you made the decision and you'll want to buy as many as you can. After making this commitment to invest, I bet the only regret you will have is that you didn't commit sooner.

- 2 -

LEARN

Preparation is essential. For many people, this is the most important component. When you prepare yourself, you can be ready for anything. A good market or a bad market. It is important to set yourself up for success. You need to educate yourself properly, put systems in place that will help you reach your goals, and practice strategies that will catapult yourself into success.

Knowledge is invaluable when it comes to being successful. You can never read enough, meet enough people, or absorb enough information. Everything that happens to you in life is either a lesson, or a blessing. Your path so far in life has shaped you to be who you are today. So take the step to educate yourself on the topics that align with your goals and aspirations, so that you can create the path that will lead you to who you want to be in the future.

There is a balance to maintain between execution, and preparation. You will never be prepared for everything that comes your way in life, but you must have the tools to deal with problems that you will incur. This will allow you to not only get through them, but come out of the other side a better person, with more knowledge ready to take on the next challenge.

A big road block that people hit is when they feel like they don't know enough to execute on their goals or dreams. They blame not executing, on their lack of knowledge. There is a point in which you will have to understand that most of what you learn will be in the process, you can only prepare so much before you have to take the plunge and learn the rest on the way, knowing when to do this can be difficult.

You may find yourself never taking that leap and letting analysis paralysis take over. Analysis paralysis is the state of over-analyzing or over-thinking a situation so that a decision or action is never taken. It is far better to jump into something with less knowledge and be willing to learn the rest on the way, than to never take that leap at all and wish you did later.

Preparing yourself with a good financial base is crucial. You may need to make a lifestyle change and evaluate your wants and your needs. There will need to be sacrifices made, but that is how you get ahead. You need to have money set aside in a reserve bank account, money that you don't touch. This money is only to fix unforeseen problems and make financial moves when necessary.

Although, having too much money sitting dormant is a bad thing. Cash is useless until you use it. Every day your cash sits in the bank it is decreasing in value because of inflation. Inflation is when prices rise and the value of money falls. The more money that is printed the less value that money has. Inflation is normal, the U.S. government is constantly printing money, making money worth less because it is less scarce. We don't notice a difference day to day, but slowly over time inflation can hurt. You need to put your cash into something that is rising with the market and economy.

Don't let every dollar you save sit idly. Create an emergency account with 3-6 months of living expenses that you don't touch and invest everything else. This account is just in case you take on an unforeseen financial burden. After stashing away your emergency fund, take your left over cash and put it to work. Invest this money in whatever you feel is right for you. The most important thing is that you keep your money growing with the market so you don't fall behind. Many people put their savings in a money market account. A money market account is an interest bearing account much like a savings account but typically gives a higher return. One of my favorite money market accounts is from

Capital One. They give a 2% annual return for a balance of $10,000 or more, have no fees and they are insured by the FDIC. 2% may not seem like a lot, but it is very generous compared to other savings accounts. This 2% return will keep your money growing slowly but surely.

Creating a budget is the first step in investing in your future. Start by understanding where your money is going at any moment. Find out how much money you spend each month, and where. This doesn't mean to think about it and say "hmm… I spend a lot of money eating out". This means, print out your bank statements for the last 2 months and put your purchases into categories such as; groceries, rent or mortgage, eating out, luxuries, bills, and so on. I use an app called "Mint" to track my expenses. It links to your bank account and automatically categorizes all spending and sends you updates of how much you're spending on each category. This app has saved me thousands.

This will open your eyes to exactly what your future will look like if you keep living the way you are now. The key in this is to find the 'one thing'. This is the thing that you thought wasn't a big deal, but actually is. Almost everyone has one. You will see that $10 Starbucks trip every morning is costing you $300/mo, eating out is costing you $400/mo, and that gym membership you forgot about is costing you $100/mo. These things will eat you alive. You need to be in your bank account every single day to take a mental snapshot of what is coming in and out.

Here's a scary reality for you. Let's say you spend $3 at Starbucks every day for a year. After reading this book you stop and decide to save that $3 every day. In one year, that savings would be able to buy you a $200,000 piece of real estate with $100 left over. This may seem unlikely, but trust me i've done it, and after reading this book, you will too.

Now ask yourself, would you rather have a Starbucks every day? Or a piece of real estate that will continue to make you money for the rest of your life? If you chose Starbucks, this may not be the book for you.

Realistically, you can't create a large savings cushion by saving $3 a day. You need to change your mindset, take a step back and look at what changes you can make in your lifestyle that will allow you to put more money aside and get you where you need to be. You need to understand where your money is going every month. Create a realistic goal, a dollar amount that you can set aside every month for your cushion. This cushion will create some piece of mind for you, knowing you have a plan B if things go south. This cushion will also allow you to throw money around when you need to. When you come across a deal you can't pass up, you can jump on it.

When the market takes a downturn and you don't have a cushion saved up, you will be crippled. When the market takes a downturn and you have a savings, this is when you really make moves.

A good market can reward the bad players. In a good market, life is good, people are making money because people are spending money. Everyone is happy while buying things they may ordinarily not be able to afford. This is called "over-leveraging", using credit to buy things you could not sustain in a bad market. A good market can be great for everyone. Let's talk about what happens in a bad market. Those that over-leverage in a good market, now have to sell what they have because they can't afford to keep it now that business has slowed down. That $30,000 boat that you bought is now only worth $20,000 and you still owe $25,000 on it leaving you upside down. In a bad market, the 'A' players make their moves.

When people buy too much in a good market like a house that is above their means, they will be forced to sell it when the market crashes. Are they going to get top dollar for their house? No. They will sell it for nothing because they have no choice, they need to sell it fast or it will be in foreclosure. Thankfully you are smart and saved your money because in this market, instead of selling your house, you are now buying homes. Instead of panicking, smart players choose this bad market as a time to make moves. When you play in this bad market and the market turns good again, that's where the real money is made.

This doesn't mean to wait until a bad market to start buying homes. I've seen people purchase amazing deals in an amazing market and I've seen people buy horrible deals in a horrible market. The truth of the matter is that nobody knows if the market is going to go up down left or sideways, you need to be in the market to make money, bottom line.

The key to good preparation is ensuring you have backup funds to properly cover yourself in a time of need, or execute on that next business endeavor and gain the knowledge you need to invest like a champion. Always remember, preparation without execution will get you nothing.

Imagine life exactly how you want it, and reverse engineer how to get there. Many people focus on how they are going to become financially free. They become fixated on the process.

Nothing in your plan will come about exactly how you want it to or imagined it to. If it did, you'd already be rich and famous as a future telling guru. Things happen every day that nobody would ever expect. When getting into real estate, you have to have ambition and determination, mixed with some realistic expectations. In real estate, there is a long game and a short game. People start investing at 18 years old and people start investing at 70 years old. There isn't a right or wrong way to do it, just different ways to do it.

To a lot of people, real estate investing sounds like a huge expensive high power job. Many people hear it and think that they'll never be able to do it. Anything is possible. Your mindset can have a huge impact on what you're future will look like. Those who stay fearful and never get started will live just like that, fearful. Those who take the leap and execute on their dreams are the ones who deserve to be rewarded with the success and riches that come with investing in real estate.

Before you start, you need to focus on one thing. Your 'why'. Your 'why' is the reason you're doing what you're doing. The reason you picked this book up. The reason you want to be successful and grow passive income streams. The reason you want to get ahead instead of staying in the 9-5 pocket. There may be many reasons; paying for your children's college education, retiring early, buy your parents a house, buy that Ferrari, Bentley or Rolls-Royce you've always dreamed of, or simply growing an income stream that your family can enjoy for generations. Whatever your 'why' is. Define it. Once defined, write it down and post it somewhere where you will see it every day. Never forget the reason you work so hard. It's important to stay motivated, but also stay humble.

Mindset will have a huge impact on your degree of success. Statistically, your net worth will be +/- 10% of what your parents' net worth is. Simply because this is what you know. This is how you have been raised and you will generally do close to the same things your parents have done simply by being in that environment your whole life.

Subconsciously, your mind is striving to be like your mom and/or dad and at some point you will. This isn't bad or negative. This is just showing how important your environment is to the outcome of your life. Same goes with your friend group. If you surround yourself with bad people, odds are you will end up doing bad things. If you hang out with entrepreneurs, odds are you will become more entrepreneurial. In order to break this, you need to not only think bigger, but whole heartedly believe you will be as successful as you wish. Change the way you think and talk. Instead of saying "I want to be a millionaire by the time I'm 30" change that to "I will be a millionaire by the time I'm 30". You will be surprised the amount of impact this has on your life.

Thinking theses positive thoughts about your future can shape what your future will actually look like. Every time a negative thought comes into your head, acknowledge it, and change it to be something positive. After a while you will hardwire your brain to start thinking more positive thoughts instead of negative ones. This doesn't happen overnight, but if you take the steps to change negative thoughts every day, you will in turn decrease the amount of negativity flowing into your life.

Create a vision board. Get a large poster or sheet of paper and put everything you want on it. My vision board has a private jet, Bentley, Porsche, Rolex, private island, family and more. Multiple times a day I glance at this board in my office. Every time I look at it, it makes me remember why I am doing what I'm doing. This small uplift will keep you propelled toward your goals and keep you heading in the right direction.

The law of attraction is the belief that your negative and positive thoughts can create negative and positive experiences. As Shakespeare says "There is nothing either good or bad, thinking makes it so". This means that your mind can determine whether something is good or bad. Not the event that took place.

All emotions that we feel, we created from our own thoughts and experiences. If you have a family member die, it can be tragic and change your life forever. You can become depressed, and this event can easily turn your life upside down. Where in some cultures, the death of a person is not looked at to be negative, but positive. They look at death as just another step in your souls journey. If you get in a car accident, you can easily be mad, sad, or depressed. You can also just as easily be happy that you survived and can now appreciate life in a different way. Nothing that happens in your life is good or bad. It's only your mind that tells you something is good or bad. You need to stay positive and hardwire your mind to stay optimistic even when it seems like things aren't going the way you want them to, or thought they would. Yes, these are extreme examples, but they show the power of the mind and how we have been conditioned to think a certain way, without even knowing it.

Investing can be a whirlwind. It is incredibly important to stay positive and always look at the bright side no matter how hard it is. If you break easily, this may not be the career for you. There will be plenty of times that you get rejected, ignored, or told no. Every time this happens you need to look at it positively. Every 'no' you get, just means you're closer to the next 'yes'.

Real estate is best played as a long game. If you lose motivation it will cripple you. When I first started in real estate I was living in my in-laws extra bedroom cold calling people all day long. Getting yelled at, being told "no" from 8am-6pm for weeks. I called hundreds and hundreds of people, without exaggeration. I never got a deal from that. Not one single person wanted to list their house with me. I was a failure in every sense of the word. It would have been so easy to give up after that. Luckily, instead of looking at this experience as horrible or a waste of time. It taught me to double down on my strengths. Maybe I'm not very good at phone interactions, maybe I'm not saying the right things. These calls gave me hundreds of opportunities to learn how to interact with people I don't know and learn how to communicate with people in the real estate world. After making these calls and being told "no" so much. I am no longer phased by it. It taught me to brush it off and move on. It also taught me the importance of asking. You never know the answer until you ask.

I want to make sure when you put this book down, you can come out swinging. By the end of this book you will have the tools and knowledge to talk to any investor or real estate professional and know what you're talking about. You will have the confidence to acquire your first real estate deal and have the tools to create lasting wealth with that deal that you and your family can enjoy for a lifetime. You will have a plan to escape the rat race, retire whenever you want, and truly be financially free. Before we dive into real estate specifically, I want to go over investing as a whole. After this next chapter, you will understand the different investment vehicles available, which vehicle works best for who, why they choose them, and why real estate is in my opinion the best way to invest.

- 3 -

INVESTING

Investing by definition is the act of committing money or capital to an endeavor with the expectation of obtaining an additional income or profit. Investing is a key component to success and financial freedom. It's near impossible to work and save money to eventually become a multi-millionaire. You have to work for your money and also have your money work for you. Before we begin, I would like to shed some light on the world of investing so you can better understand investing as a whole and why people do it. When investing, there is a trade off, riskier investments have the potential to have a bigger reward. Less risky investments generally have a lower reward. The key to investing is to have time and to be patient. The more time your money is invested, the more time your money has to grow.

You can invest in anything from baseball cards to antique cars, but there are a few investment vehicles everyone should learn about; stocks, bonds, mutual funds, and real estate. Let's dive in to each one so you can really understand how to best use these different investment vehicles.

The stock market as a whole is the collection of markets and exchanges where the issuing and trading of equities (stocks of publicly held companies) and other types of securities takes place. The stock market trades in a few different places. One being the New York Stock Exchange. This exchange has some of the worlds largest corporations, usually known as blue chip stocks. Blue chip stocks are stocks that are generally safe. They have a good track record of rising in the long term. Most of the trading at the NYSE is done face-to-face. The NASDAQ is a market that trades entirely online. They flow through most online brokerages that most investors know today. Those are the two popular exchanges most people trade on. You can always buy a single stock from a company on one of these platforms, or for a more well rounded portfolio you can buy a collection of securities through a mutual fund.

Mutual funds are essentially just pools of money provided by fellow investors or companies, all used to buy a collection of stocks. Many mutual funds have different strategies and purposes. Mutual funds can be one of the easier and more stress free ways to invest and tend to attract lots of new investors for that reason. They are usually well balanced and typically include very established companies. The biggest advantage of a mutual funds is the diversification. One single fund can have securities from thousands of issuers. This mitigates your potential loss immensely. Mutual funds generally grow slow but steady over time which make them great for the long term. Although a long term investment, your money is still semi-liquid. Shares in a mutual fund can be bought or sold any day the market is open, Monday-Friday with the exception of holidays.

Bonds are simple debt investments. Essentially, you are letting a company or state borrow money from you. Different entities use these to refinance debt they currently have, take on new projects, or to float them in their existing operations. As interest rates rise or drop, bonds are bought and sold. Because you are supplying the debt and not taking the debt on, you want the highest interest rate possible. If you buy a $1,000 bond at 6% and interest rates drop to 5%, the bond will continue paying out at 6%, this is considered an 'attractive bond'. Investors will buy up these bonds, in turn bidding the price up until the effective rate, or 'market rate' equals 5%. If the interest rate rises to 7%, your bond is now unattractive because you can buy a new bond that would yield you 1% more. In this case the bond price will decrease to sell at a discount until the effective rate is 6% thus trying again to purchase a bond above market interest rates.

In simple terms, bonds go up and down based on demand. The more bonds sold, the lower the interest rate will be. Put it this way, if your company really needed $100,000 to start a new project, you'd be willing to pay a higher interest rate to get that money. Let's say 7%. After you've gathered that $100,000 everything else is a surplus. You're not going to pay a premium interest rate to your investors for any amount over $100,000 because you don't really need that money. You'll probably drop the rate to 4% or 5%. As people sell their bonds and your holdings become less, you'll want to raise the interest rate enticing more people to buy to get an influx of usable capital. This is simple supply and demand.

When investing in stocks, there are two different markets, the primary market and the secondary market. The primary market is where new shares are initially sold when a company goes public. When a company goes 'public' it is called an IPO (Initial Public Offering). Institutional investors generally buy most of these up from investment banks. All trading after this goes to the secondary market where institutional investors and individual investors like you and me both trade. Buying stocks is as easy as finding a company you like and setting up an investment account.

Setting up an investment account can be as simple as going to your local Scottrade or Edward Jones branch and having them do the work. I am much more of a do it yourself guy so my favorite way to invest in stocks is to use TD Ameritrade. They have a very intuitive app and everything is hands on.

I only invest in what I like and use personally. I like to be in charge of my investments. Bigger firms will move your money around and sometimes require a monthly deposit into your investment account, plus you have to pay them a commission. With TD, it is all done online with no commission, it's just a $10 fee per trade no matter how much you're trading. Although you are in charge of your own portfolio, the SEC (U.S. Securities and exchange commission) has strict guidelines in place to discourage certain actions like day trading, so these independent companies set limits on how often you can buy and sell your stocks.

Day trading is a strategy that some people have become extremely successful at. This is when you watch many different stocks in real time and buy and sell as they fluctuate in value. This is most effective when you have a lot of money to start with. If you buy 1,000 shares of Sony at $40 per share, you pay $40,000. If in that day, hour, or minute, the stock goes up to $41 per share, which can be likely, your stock holding is now worth $41,000. You will then pull your money out and you just made $1,000 by watching the stock and pulling out at the right time. You will then put this $40,000 back into another stock and do the same thing. This risky arbitrage can be incredibly rewarding, but there is a lot of legality behind it.

I've known people who have become very successful in this, but there are a lot of things to know before getting into it, there are balance minimums and trading maximums along with many other rules created by the SEC to keep everyones money safe. Day trading can be incredibly risky and is a bit more like gambling than investing. It takes a lot of market knowledge and guts to pull this off. For every person who has made a fortune doing this, there are 100 people who have lost a lot of money. The SEC has these certain guidelines in place to make sure people are being responsible and not abusing the securities system.

When you buy a stock from a company you are in turn buying a piece of that company. For instance, all electronic devices I use are from Apple. Therefore, I buy stock in Apple. If I truly believe in the company enough to buy their stuff year after year, why not get a piece of their profits? I have invested in companies that I haven't had first hand experience with, but a general rule of thumb is if you're a customer, become an owner too. When I first started investing in stocks I fell in love. I worked at a small coffee shop and I didn't have too much money to put in, but every day I watched how the stocks were performing and many days I made a few extra dollars on top of my initial investment. No matter the amount of money, it's really nice to know that even when you're sitting on the couch, your money is working for you, growing slowly but surely.

While investing can be fun and a good way to make money, it is important to define what a good investment is. The stock market has historically given an ROI (return on investment) of about 10% each year. This means if you put $1,000 into the stock market you will on average make $100 or 10% in one year. This data is based on historical evidence from the S&P 500 index which is comprised of around 500 of Americas largest traded companies.

Investing is best played with a long term mindset. If you can, never sell until you really feel like you need to. Don't let emotions get involved when making the decision to sell your investments. You always lose money when you sell. Let's say you buy 100 shares of a stock at $100.00 a share. In the next 2 months, the stock goes down to $80.00 a share. You panic and sell your shares for a loss because you don't want it to go any lower. This is exactly what not to do. Inflation proves that if the company itself is stable, it will eventually go up. Maybe not tomorrow, but it will. You just lost $2,000 because of your emotions getting in the way.

Even if you made money, you still usually lose potential profit when you sell. If your portfolio grew from $10,000 to $100,000 in 20 years and you decide to sell. Odds are that your portfolio would've grown another $100,000 in the next 20 years as well. You pulled out and made $90,000 when you could've waited another 20 years and pulled out $190,000. This is what I mean when I say that you always lose money when you sell. It isn't always a bad thing to sell your investments to realize profits that you've made. It is just something to consider when doing so. I don't get bright eyed when I see a large number in my investment portfolio and I don't sell unless I need to or know in my gut it's the right time to pull out. When I do sell, I don't go out and buy something flashy, I will usually put that money back into another investment of some kind so it can continue to grow.

Since the year 1900, on average, there is a correction every year. A correction is when the market drops down

10%-19.99% (a 20% fall is considered a bear market or what most people call a "crash") 80% of these corrections, never become a bear market. A bear market on average happens every 5-10 years. An average fall for a bear market is 33%, and will last about one year. Remember, you only lose 33% if you sell. If and when this bear market hits, you have to be prepared to hold on tight and not let your emotions get in the way, trust the market and your money will be made whole again.

The only thing you can do that is worse than selling your portfolio for a loss, is to be out of the market. You can only make money if you are in the market. You can watch form the sidelines and it can be fun, but until you are playing in the game, you will never get the reward. Unless you're betting on a zombie apocalypse, you will make money buying solid stocks from reputable companies that have been analyzed and proven to have a good track record. Never invest any money that you may need soon or can't afford to lose. Don't over-leverage yourself and invest all of your savings because when your car breaks down and your stock happens to be down at the same time, you'll be forced to sell for a loss.

Fear and investing do not compliment each other, they are a volatile mix. Being a fearful investor is being a bad investor. It is important to remember, never overreact to anything in the market, it fluctuates a lot day to day. Don't check your numbers every second and let it determine your mood. It will go up and it will go down, you have to think long term when investing. Don't blame the market when your stock dips and you pulled out. Of course you have to balance it out with a level of caution. You can't just buy a bunch of random stocks and hope they will double in 2 years. Do your research and be patient.

Patience is extremely important when investing. One of the biggest financial decisions you can make today is to decide to invest. If you decide that stock investing is something you would like to do, a good way to start is to create a routine and make a promise to yourself. Pick a dollar amount and put that money to work. No matter how much it is, find a number and put that number into the market every month. Be it $10, or $10,000. Automate it so you don't even see it. Put it in an investment account. If you don't think you have the money to do this, look at it this way, if your rent or mortgage payment was $20 more, you would still pay it right? You would find a way. This is how you really grow your investments and create a strong investment account with great future returns.

I hope this helps you better understand the power that investing has. There are many different ways to invest, you just need to evaluate your options and choose an investing vehicle that is right for you. There is a big dilemma when investing. One half of people will tell you to diversify, which means to not invest solely in one thing. They say to invest in different markets so if one drastically falls, you will have another one that stays in good shape. Whereas if you had all of your eggs in one basket and that market falls, you lose everything in that basket.

The other half of people will tell you to invest in what you know. Only invest in what you truly understand. Don't buy

$20,000 in Disney stock just because your friend told you to. You need to dive into the company as a whole, understand where they are in the market, where they have been, and where they will likely be going. Before investing in anything you must understand it or you might as well be putting money at the roulette table because you aren't investing, you're gambling. There are no right or wrong ways to invest, just different ways. I can only share what I have seen and learned from experience. I have studied finance and economics for a long time and I have found that real estate is hands down the best way to invest for those willing to learn how. It isn't as passive as stock investing, you can't purchase a home in 5 seconds from your phone on your lunch break. But it can prove to be much more rewarding. Now, I'm going to show you why.

- 4 -

REAL ESTATE

After this section, you will understand why I went all in on real estate and did everything I could to make real estate work for me. It has been said that 85% of all millionaire and billionaires made their money through real estate. Real estate investing isn't a new thing, it has been around since the dawn of time. People have been trading land as long as there has been land to claim.

Many people invest in real estate now and you'd never know. Taylor Swift owns a ton of real estate, Brad Pitt and George Clooney bought a piece of land in Las Vegas for 90 million in 2005 and sold it in 2006 for 202 million. They made a 112 million dollar profit in one year, on one transaction. Vanilla Ice is an avid real estate investor and even had his own show on the DIY network. Shaq has a real estate portfolio worth just over 52 million now and climbing.

These are just a few examples of people who are on the right track. A persons house is usually the biggest and most expensive asset they will buy in their lifetime. Everyone needs a place to live, so why not capitalize on it?

If you are truly interested in investing in real estate I highly recommend you make the first step and get your real estate license. It is not as hard as it sounds. You sign up for a course online, after about 3 months worth of studying, you take a big test and if you pass, you're done. Setting that time aside to get your license can multiply your future income and take your investment game to a new level.

Not only does getting your real estate license teach you all about the real estate world and the legality behind buying and selling property. It also allows you to make more money on every deal that you do.

There are many real estate investors that don't have their license and don't want to get it. My recommendation is to not quit your day job and become a realtor right off the bat. If you want to buy real estate and can't pay cash for the whole thing like most people, you'll need a lender. The lender will not approve your loan if you don't have enough income on paper. When you're a real estate agent you are technically self employed. Mortgage companies look at that and need minimum 2 years of calendar income from your real estate profession, or any self employed profession. The lender will take your income from these two years and lend to you based on the average income you made out of those two years. If you have a day job, keep it and spend every moment you aren't at work, working on real estate deals until it replaces your current income and you are happy. It can take years to become a successful full time real estate agent. Just like anything, it takes time, so be patient. Play safe, keep your day job and use that income to help get funding for your deals. Try not to switch professions either as it can have an impact in the lenders eyes if you haven't been employed by the same employer for a solid length of time. The lenders want to know that you have a stable long term job that will pay the mortgage every month so they can get their money back. They don't want to see you jump from random job to random job, this looks unstable in their minds.

For those fresh in the real estate world, I'm going to explain how real estate agents work and where their income comes from.

(A quick disclaimer, lots of real estate guidelines are state specific. Although many rules and regulations are the same, there may be different nuances. If you have any questions, ask your local real estate board. I will be writing from experience in California.)

After receiving your real estate license, you must hang your license with a broker. The broker holds the liability for you in case you make any mistakes along your journey. You will spend your first few months with your broker just training and learning the ropes of real estate.

The way that you get paid is through commission. Every house you help someone buy or sell, you get a cut of. It varies, but typically 3% per sale for one side of the transaction. That means if you help someone buy a home, you get 3% of that homes selling price. If you help someone sell their home, you get 3% of the selling price, only after the home is officially sold and the buyers have their keys.

Let's say someone wants to sell their house for $200,000. The seller has to pay 6% in commission. That means just to sell their home, they have to pay $12,000 in commissions. $6,000 goes to the person trying to sell the home and $6,000 goes to the person who ends up bringing the buyer. Not in every state, but in California you can do something that is called a 'double ended sale'. This is when you as an agent represent both the buyer and seller of the home.

For example, this same person approaches you and wants you to list their house. (List is just another term for sell, it essentially means 'listing it on the MLS' which is the multiple listing service, an online collective of all homes for sale that generally only agents get access to.) You list this persons house for $200,000. It's up for sale and you're waiting for an agent to come with a buyer, but instead of an agent brining a buyer, you know someone who wants to buy the house. You skip the buying agent and do all the paperwork yourself. This will result in you getting the entire 6% commission for the sale. You get $12,000 for simply listing the house for sale, and finding someone to buy it yourself.

This can be a grey area in real estate because as an agent you have the fiduciary duty to unbiasedly help represent your client. When your clients are both buying the home and selling the home, negotiating can be though. Odds are, you know the sellers bottom dollar that they will sell the home for and you can't tell the buyer that. You will also know what the buyer is per-approved for which is exactly how much he or she can afford to spend. You can see how this can be a little bit shady. That's why it isn't allowed in all states.

Being a real estate agent can also hold other perks as well in the form of referrals. When you're an agent, word of mouth will eventually bring family, friends and even friends of friends to you wanting to buy or sell homes. If someone approaches you wanting to buy a home and you don't have the time or want to service them, you can refer them to another agent. This referral can bring you 10-50% of the deal. This is another business entirely on its own. If someone approaches you wanting to sell their property, but you're too busy doing other things or just don't want to go through that process. You can contact another agent you know and trust and tell them you have someone who is interested in selling their home and you'll give them their information for a 25% cut of the commission, as long as the sellers are willing of course. The agent will be glad to do it because that's a deal they never would have had before. After all, for them 75% of a deal is better than 100% of no deal.

When this house closes, you will get 25% of their commission for doing nothing and the agent will get 75% (minus their broker fees) for helping the client. This is a win win scenario. Working a full time job this can be a great way to make extra money with almost no effort at all, just linking buyers and sellers with agents.

By the commissions earned, you can see how it can be very lucrative having your real estate license. If you ever buy or sell a home one time in your life, the license will pay for itself many times over. Many people don't have their license to buy and sell homes for other people, they just use it for their own transactions to increase profit. Not only does the license teach you a lot about the world of real estate, it also allows you to make more on every deal that you do by getting that commission, even on the homes you buy yourself. If the house you're trying to purchase is on the MLS, it should have a commission amount tied to it. As an agent, you can see how much commission you will get back by buying a property. This can be incredibly rewarding, especially when the market is high and deals become scarce.

Do yourself a favor and get your real estate license, make this the first step toward your goal of being financially free. After it's done, you will thank me every single time you do a deal. You don't have to go head on into being a real estate agent. But when you have it, it's easy to do a few deals a year for friends and family bringing you a few extra thousand every year. There's no schedule when you're an agent, no boss telling you what to do all the time. It's up to you, how far you want to take it.

Investing in real estate can mean a couple of different things. Flipping, buy and hold, wholesaling and note investing just to name a few. Most of us have at least heard the term flipping before.

Flipping can be very rewarding, but always boils down to buying the home at the right price. This is crucial and has put many people in serious trouble. We've all heard of or seen the shows where someone or some couple buys a home for $100,000, put a few thousand into it, has a bunch of people work on it, and magically it is worth $200,000. This is all great, but it is never this easy. Because of this trend, there are too many people trying to do this, so finding deals can be hard and you have to get creative. The awesome thing about fixing and flipping is something I call sweat equity.

Equity is the money that your house is worth above your mortgage, or what you owe. If your home is worth $200,000 and you still owe $150,000 to the lender. That means you have $50,000 in equity. Sweat equity is a great way to make your home worth more, without putting a bunch of money into it. Sweat equity basically just means that you are putting your own time, blood, sweat, and tears into fixing your house up to make it worth more. Not spending a bunch of money on a contractor to have him do the work. In reality, with the internet and all of the other resources available, you could learn how to tile a bathroom in about an hour. This is what many people do if they don't have a lot of capital to put into their home, they just do it themselves.

Flipping can be a great way to make some good money, but you have to know a lot. Not only about houses and construction, but the market and area that you are flipping in. Flipping can simply be to buy a home, fix it up and sell it for a profit. Or it can be buying a piece of land, landscaping it, clear cutting trees and selling it for a profit.

If you can't find good deals, you have to make good deals. Finding a good deal can be tough, you can turn an average deal into a great deal with just a bit of knowledge and creativity. Here are a few creative methods I've learned that have proven to be valuable. Many of these can be used as flipping or buy and hold techniques. First, search the MLS or Zillow and find a house that is a 2/2, two bedrooms and two bathrooms that has over 1,100 square feet. The trick with this is that 1,100 square feet for a 2/2 is pretty large. Odds are that you can get a basic permit, put up a wall, and add a 3rd bedroom. The difference between a 2/2 and a 3/2 in price can be a lot. In some areas it can yield another

$100,000. This is an easy way to create value in a single family home.

Another creative way is to add an extra room above a garage. Generally the attic of a garage is pretty bare, not a lot going on up there. Investors will chop the top off the roof of the garage and make it structurally sound. After doing this they will add another bonus room or living space above that garage sometimes adding 500 square feet to the home. This is what I mean when I say you need to get creative to add value to a home.

You can also convert the garage into a bedroom or two. I've seen someone convert a 2 car garage into 2 bedrooms bringing a house form a 3 bedroom to a 5 bedroom. Let's say you live in a college town and you have a 3 bedroom house that is renting for $750 per bedroom. The three rooms would yield you $2,250 per month. You convert the garage and add two more bedrooms. Doing this all in all costs you a whopping $20,000. Seems like a lot huh? Now that you're extra bedrooms are built and renting, you're brining in another $18,000 per year off those two bedrooms. This will pay itself off after just a year and 2 months. After that, it's pure profit. You're brining yourself another $1,500 every month.

But how could you afford a $20,000 garage remodel after you just bought a house? Take out a loan. These are capital investments and there's nothing scary about taking on a little debt to further your financial yield. I wouldn't recommend doing this, but let's say you paid this entire $20,000 remodel on a credit card with 25% interest. It would take just about a year and a half to pay off the entire balance of the credit card and interest.

To win in this game you have to get creative. A big component when flipping is making money 'on the buy'. Which means to buy the property under market value so you could instantly sell it after buying it and still clear a profit.

When flipping, it is important to understand where trends are. Many people like very open living spaces, clean lines and light colored interiors. It's important to add only components that will add value and that people want. Don't go and replace every single window in the home. People don't care about windows as much as they do the flooring or master bathroom. Make sure you understand what your end buyer would want before you start the project.

My favorite type of real estate investment is the buy and hold method. Meaning, buying a property, renting it out, and holding it for a long period of time. If you buy a house for $150,000. Your mortgage will be about $800. When investing in buy and hold rental properties, the property should rent for no less than 1% of the purchase price. Let's say in your area a $150,000 home rents for $1,500 per month. That's an extra $700 you are taking home every month in profit because your rent income is $1,500, your mortgage to pay on that property is $800. So $1,500 - $800 = $700 in cash flow coming to you every month just from renting out the house. These numbers are hard to get, especially on the west and east coast. It is tough, but not impossible. You really have to put the work in on the front end to find the best deals. Let's look at the long term.

Over time your house will appreciate. Which means it will go up in value, because of inflation. Fast forward 10 years. Your $150,000 home, is now worth $200,000. Just by owning the home, not only have you collected an extra $700 every month for ten years, and had someone paying your mortgage payment for you while gaining that equity, but you've also made an extra $50,000 on your investment.

The buy and hold method takes patience, but can build your net worth enormously. No matter what price, style, or location of house you buy, if you rent it out for 30 years, that's free money. Someone else paid the mortgage for 30 years and every single month added money to your net worth. One of the easiest ways to become a millionaire is to incur $1,000,000 worth of real estate debt and have someone pay it off for you over time by renting out the property (or properties). This is not at all as hard as it sounds, it just takes patience.

Wholesaling is another great strategy to get started in real estate. Many people do this to start their journey in the business.

It takes no money to start, just time and effort. There is a bit of legality behind it. If you're thinking of becoming a wholesaler, please do your research to make sure what you are doing is not only ethical, but legal. This process requires you to have great negotiation and marketing skills. You also need to have a good understanding of a houses worth, and ARV or After Repair Value (the value of a property after it has been repaired and is in good sellable condition).

Wholesaling essentially means that you are supplying real estate investors with good deals. This doesn't take a real estate license or anything fancy, you just need a good deal to start. You make your money on a "finders fee". You simply find a good deal, bring it to an investor, mark up the price and give him the deal.

Let's say you do some networking and marketing in your local area. You find someone who doesn't want to pay all the fees that a real estate agent charges and just want's to get rid of the home. It's in bad condition and the seller doesn't want to deal with inspections, contractors, and the overall headache that is fixing up a house. They just want to unload it.

You travel to this persons house and you decide any investor would buy it for $150,000 based on what you know about the market. You tell the potential seller that you will buy the home for $130,000. They agree. You now have the seller sign a purchase contract with you saying that you will buy the property, or find someone to buy the property within a certain period of time. Let's say 14 days. You network some more and find a local investor, you tell your investor that you have a great deal in the pipeline and show him the house. You tell him that you'll sell the house to him for $150,000 ($20,000 more than you previously agreed with the seller), the investor takes the deal. You then sign an assignment contract with the investor giving him rights to purchase the home and he's off to the races. You don't do anything else but collect the difference. You just made $20,000 buy finding a good deal.

Investors have slowly become weary of wholesalers. They have a certain stigma of being shady. Doing whatever it takes to find a deal, taking advantage of people and lying to investors to get them to buy a deal. As an investor, never take anyones word for an ARV. You need to analyze the property yourself and find out what you need to buy the house at to make the numbers work. Never trust any numbers but your own. Along this same line, never trust anyones word about condition. I've seen people buy houses that had paint over dry rot to cover it up, lattice covering a cracked footing, holes in walls covered by mirrors. Trust nobody, do your due diligence.

Not all wholesalers are bad. There are many out there making an honest living and are dang good at it. They know how to market and they know how to network. Having a good relationship with a wholesaler can be invaluable, there is nothing better than having someone out looking for deals on your side keeping your pipeline full, so you can concentrate on growing your portfolio and business.

Note investing can be very rewarding for someone who wants to invest passively. This is a great method for someone who doesn't have the time, energy or know-how to invest in real estate physical property.

Note investing is when you buy the debt of the homeowner and become the new lender. This "note" we're talking about is a short term for promissory note. A promissory note is a part of any financed home, this note spells out all of the terms of the loan and holds the buyer to their asset, the house. Notes can be bought and sold in a few different fashions. Let's start with performing and non-performing notes.

A performing note is when a homeowner has paid all of their payments and has done nothing wrong, but the lender wants out. The lender can want out for many reasons the most common reason is that the lender doesn't want to wait for the loan to mature in 15 or 30 years, they want their cash back now. These are typically individuals or companies who have owner financed a property or properties and just want their cash back to put into other deals.

Non-performing notes and loans that have been left unpaid. The homeowner has come on hard times and stopped paying their mortgage. If a bank of company has a lot of these, they may want to unload them at a discount instead of going through the lengthy and costly foreclosure process.

Note investing is great because no matter what you will usually make money. Let me explain. John owns a house in Texas, the home is worth $200,000. He has stopped paying his payment and the bank wants to wash their hands of him. He still owes $150,000 on the home. The bank sells the note to you for $100,000. You call up the homeowner and tell them the situation. You tell them you are here to help. Note investing can be extremely rewarding for both the investor and the homeowner. You talk to him and find out that he just needs a month to get his life together and he will start paying again. Maybe you even help him out and say you'll lower his mortgage payment $100 to help him out. He owes $150,000 so let's say his new payment is $1,000. You are now being paid $1,000 per month on your $100,000 investment. Over the course of 30 years you will bring in $360,000 in payments from him. That's pretty good for not having to deal with tenant evictions, liabilities, broken toilets and emergency calls.

If this tenant isn't ready to make a deal and doesn't want to pay, you'll have to foreclose on him. This sounds bad but really isn't. For some notes it's the best case scenario. Let's say all in you have to pay $20,000 to foreclose on the house and get it in selling condition. You own this property for $100,000 because that's what the bank sold the note to you for. We have already established the house is worth $200,000. All in on the property you've paid $120,000. $100,000 for the note and $20,000 for the eviction/rehab. You sell the house for market value at $200,000 after agent fees and taxes you could walk away with an easy $50,000.

There is much more that goes into this process than buying a note and collecting money. There is legal work to be done and you have to watch your back for things like liens and location. Different states have different laws for financing property and buying and selling notes. Like any investment type, do your research and make sure above all, that you and your money are as protected as you can be.

With real estate you need to be flexible. You have to change and evolve with the market. In fast appreciating markets flipping can be very profitable, in steady markets buy and holds can be a more fruitful option. There is no right answer to what you should invest in or how you should invest. Find out what direction you want to take in life and decide what method will best take you there. A well rounded investor can make money in any location, in any market cycle, you just have to know what dollars to deploy and where. It's not impossible, once equipped with the knowledge, you will be unstoppable.

- 5 -

GET FUNDING

Before diving into the real estate investment world you need to define your goals and create a map to get yourself there. I will help every step of the way. Before you purchase anything, you need to define your goals and secure the money to meet those goals.

Find that number that you want and do anything and everything it takes to get there. It's simple. Let's say your goal is to generate $30,000 per month in passive income. Passive income is income or cash flow that comes in from an external source that takes little or no time or effort from you. This is money that is constantly flowing to you on a regular basis regardless of where you are or what you are doing in your life.

If your goal is $30,000 then all you need to do is break it down. For simplicity, let's say you need to have 30 people pay you $1,000 every month to make $30,000 per month. Real estate can do this for you through income properties, or better known rental properties. A rental property is a piece of real estate that you buy and rent out for more than your mortgage amount. Your mortgage amount is the amount of money you have to pay to a mortgage company to borrow the money to buy a home. These rental properties can be regular single family houses in a neighborhood. They can be duplexes, which are 2 smaller homes connected to one another. Triplexes or quadraplexes which are just 3 or 4 home units connected to each other. There is also another beast, the apartment complex.

Anything more than 4 home units connected to each other is considered commercial. Commercial rental properties can be very rewarding, but my favorite are residential rental properties simply because there is typically less turn around with people moving in and out. With smaller apartments and cheaper living spaces you tend to have people coming and going quickly which will eat into the cashflow you're receiving and cause more time and headache on your end.

An attractive aspect of investing in real estate is that you can use leverage to buy real estate investments. Leverage simply means you are using someone else's money instead of yours. You can't purchase stocks or bonds on a credit card. With real estate, you can buy a $200,000 investment property for anywhere from $0-200,000. Usually banks require you to put 20% of the purchase price down in cash, but there are many ways to get around this.

To better understand how the loan process works when buying a home I will outline a few different types of loans or mortgages available to you.

There are many loan types, the most popular being; VA, FHA, USDA, and Conventional loans. All of these loans require you to live in the property and have it be your primary residence. Conventional loans are the only loan that lets you buy non owner occupied houses. There are a few ways to get around this, but please make sure you consult your mortgage broker before you make any loan decisions. They will be able to help make the right choice for you while staying in the guidelines that these loan organizations put into place.

VA loans are for veterans. These are loans issued to borrowers who have served our country and in turn, the government guarantees these loans to the banks. So if the borrower doesn't pay his mortgage, instead of the bank losing money, the government steps in and takes care of the costs. Thus giving banks incentive to loan to veterans. Another helpful aspect of VA loans is that they offer 100% financing. Which means you don't have to have any money to put as a down payment. You will have to pay some closing costs, but if you have a good real estate agent you're working with, you can get around this too by wrapping the closing costs into the loan. I'll explain more about this later.

FHA stands for Federal Housing Administration, it is very similar to VA except it is mainly focused toward first time home buyers. Although it's structured toward first time home buyers, anyone from any walk of life can get into an FHA loan if they meet the right requirements. Like the VA loan, the government still guarantees this loan in case of default. Typically the bank likes to see no less than 3.5% down initially with this FHA loan. This means you can purchase a $200,000 investment property with only $7,000 as a down payment. This is nice for first time home buyers because they can get away with buying a house without a lot of money. One caveat with FHA loans is that you can't buy a piece of junk house. The house has to be in good condition and habitable. The mortgage company will want to do an appraisal to cover their butts in case you don't pay.

An appraisal is a process where a licensed appraiser goes out to look at the home to see exactly what the home is worth using certain metrics such as other home sales of houses near by and of the same type. They will preview the property before the loan goes through to make sure that it is truly worth what you're paying for. If you fall in love with a house and agree to pay $200,000 for the house, but every other house in that neighborhood is selling for $100,000 and your house doesn't have anything special, then you're in trouble. They are simply there to protect your and their investment. If you did go through and buy the house for $200,000 and had a loan amount of $180,000 and decided to not pay your mortgage. The company would take the home from you and sell it to get their money back. This is where the appraisal safeguard comes in. They would sell this house for $100,000 because that's what it's worth, leaving them at an $80,000 loss simply because they didn't send someone licensed out there to verify the house was truly worth what you paid for it. This process is usually required on any loan type, not just FHA.

The guidelines state that you can only do an FHA loan once. But there are a few ways to get around this if you need to.

If you can prove that you need to move because of a legitimate reason, expanding family, new job elsewhere and so on, you can get another FHA loan at 3.5% and keep your existing FHA home as a rental property. You have now gotten away with buying two houses for very little money. Although you can only do this a couple of times before the housing administration will stop granting you FHA loans. I cannot stress enough, there has to be a legitimate reason to move out of your current home. Lying to your mortgage company is considered loan fraud and can land you up to 30 years in prison. There isn't any amount of money worth that jail time. Trust me. So when getting a mortgage, talk to your loan officer and tell them your long term goals. They will be able to help you maximize your time and money to reach those goals, legally.

FHA loans can be great. On top of the great down payment option this provides, the Federal Housing Administration also created something called an FHA 203K loan. This loan will allow you to buy a fixer upper and wrap all of the renovation costs into the loan without paying anything out of pocket. This can be an extremely powerful loan. There is a lot of money to be made when fixing houses up, and not having to pay for renovation costs can be invaluable when building your rental portfolio. It is extremely important to work with a good real estate agent and mortgage broker so that they can figure out what option is best for you.

USDA loans are loans given by the United States Department of Agriculture. Yes, the same entity that certifies your meat. They have some amazing loan programs available, but only for rural agricultural development. If it is far enough from civilization, they will lend to you. This is to entice more people to get into agriculture and help stimulate that part of our economy. Many people get this mixed up and think that you have to buy a 100 acre farm in Kentucky to get this loan. Many small cities have these loans available. It is always worth a try to see if your area qualifies for this loan before locking down a mortgage type. As long as you aren't living in San Francisco or New York, odds are you aren't far from a USDA qualified property. The best thing about these USDA loans are that they require 0% down. That means you can buy a home with a $0.00 down payment.

The Department of Agriculture wants people to expand into the less populated areas, that's why they are doing this. If you ever have the option of getting this loan, jump on it. I hope you're starting to see why you don't have to be a millionaire to invest in real estate. If you have done the research yourself, or you know the right real estate agent and mortgage lender on your side, you can purchase a house for absolutely $0.00 out of your pocket. Hang in there and I'll show you how you can buy a house that qualifies for a USDA loan and actually get money back. For instance, I can buy a USDA qualified house worth $250,000 and when the purchase goes through, I actually pocket $7,500. It sounds impossible, but it isn't. Later in this chapter I'll explain exactly how you can do this.

Last but not least, conventional financing. This is your standard mortgage, typically requiring a minimum 5% down on owner occupied properties, but they mainly shoot for 20%. These loan guidelines are set by Fannie Mae and Freddie Mac which is the Federal National Mortgage Association, and the Federal Home Loan Mortgage Corporation. These are the big institutions that have strict guidelines on the money that they lend out. You can usually purchase up to four homes with these before they cut you off.

When getting a conventional loan it can be tough, after the mortgage crisis of 2008 the guidelines that Fannie Mae and Freddie Mac set are strict. There is no wiggle room. They punch your information into their algorithm and if it doesn't approve you for a mortgage, you're out of luck.

Any loan you receive by putting less than 20% down is considered a "high risk loan" and will require PMI which is private mortgage insurance. This is a monthly payment connected to your mortgage that you have to pay just in case you default on your loan. It works like this. Let's say for simplicity 10% of all home borrowers default on their loan and stop paying their mortgage. Imagine there were 100,000 loans given out by the FHA to borrowers with an average home price of $100,000. Let's say every borrower paid $100 per mont in mortgage insurance. 10% of 100,000 is 10,000. So 10,000 people stopped paying their mortgage. Which leaves 90,000 people still paying their $100 mortgage insurance every month bringing the FHA $9,000,000 every month. With the 10,000 people not paying their mortgages the FHA could lose $1,000,000,000. 10,000 people each defaulting on $100,000 loans. The FHA has a billion dollars in unpaid debt now, but they are receiving 9 million every month. This means in about 9 years the mortgage insurance paid by borrowers will pay for that 10% of people who stopped paying their mortgage.

This doesn't account for the FHA foreclosing on the homes and selling them for cash, but you can now understand how PMI works and why it's required on all high risk loans with a down payment of less than 20%. They call a borrower who puts down less than 20% high risk because they aren't putting much skin in the game. It's not hard to understand that people who don't have a lot of money are more likely to stop paying their mortgage if they have a small bump in the road or make a few bad choices.

One extremely important thing to note is that these high risk low down payment mortgage types require you to live in the property to get approved for the loan, they call these owner occupied mortgages. To get a simple mortgage on a home you are never going to live in that is strictly a rental property, you must put a minimum of 20% down. You cannot get approved for a government backed loan or high risk loan with a low down payment if you are not living in the property. If you get a government backed loan, you aren't stuck living in that property forever, but if you do get a government backed loan like an FHA, VA, or USDA, you have to fully intend to live there for at least one year sometimes more.

Some credit unions and smaller banks are portfolio lenders. A portfolio lender is a bank or lender that loans their own money. They will always have certain criteria and guidelines to stand by, but they have the power to approve you simply by their own judgment of whether or not they think you will pay back the loan. It is extremely important to build a solid relationship with a portfolio lender. They have the power to supply you with a constant stream of funding to buy properties or have a rolling loan account setup for you to be able to jump on a good deal when you see one.   Government loans and conventional loans will typically give you an absolute maximum of 10 mortgages before cutting you off. When this happens, you will be forced to get creative financing through friends and family, or find a portfolio lender who will look past your outstanding loan balances and lend you more money based on the stability of your real estate investment portfolio.

A lender will look at the sum of all the properties you have to decide if they are stable enough to give you another loan. Your real estate portfolio is a map of your history and credibility. If your lender can look at this portfolio and see that you have only purchased deals at below market value and cash flow is constant and abundant enough, they will have no problem lending to you.

There are may other ways to fund real estate deals without getting a full government mortgage such as hard money lenders. Hard money lenders are usually average people that have a surplus of money and don't want it to sit in the bank and do nothing. Most hard money lenders I've seen are past real estate investors that are tired of chasing deals and dealing with contractors or real estate agents and lenders. The later years of an investor are sometimes spent on the lending side helping those in their footsteps. It can be incredibly rewarding helping some passionate young person fulfill the same dream you had. Why not let the fresh hungry investor network, find the deals, and handle the paperwork while you kick back in Cabo and get a 12% return on your money.

There are hard money lenders everywhere that lend their own money at a specific percentage. This is often a high interest rate and you will have to pay "points" which are percentage points of the loan.

For instance, if you are buying a $300,000 home, one point would be $3,000. Typically I see most hard money lenders at around 8-12% interest and 3 points to get a loan. Hard money lenders can be extremely helpful when just starting in real estate. These lenders typically lend on the deal rather than the person. Although if they don't think you can close, you won't get the loan. Try and close every single deal you get under contract. This is a very valuable metric to a lender. They want to see that you aren't afraid and you have what it takes to get the deal done. You need to come to a hard money lender with a property and a plan. They will examine the property and determine if they can make money or not.

Hard money lenders need to make sure they are protected. If you can't pay them back, they want to know they can sell the home and at least make a few dollars for their time. Hard money lenders can be found everywhere, sometimes I think there are more hard money lenders than deals out there. As always, just make sure you vet your lender and make sure they are legitimate before doing any business transaction. If you feel you need to bring in a real estate attorney to draft up a contract then do so.

Owner carry contracts are another great option if you can't get a loan from an institutional bank. An owner carry is when the owner of the house stays on the title and you pay your monthly payment directly to the homeowner until it is payed off, then you own the house. This typically works good for someone who wants to sell a home, but doesn't need the money from it instantly. This way they can be your bank. You pay them a mortgage with interest on it. This can be great for the homeowner because they are receiving interest every month. If a homeowner does an owner carry contract at 5% for 20 years on a $200,000 house. After the loan term the owner will get his $200,000 for the home and also an additional $117,000 from interest. When you get your investment game going, this can be a great way to sell some of your properties. You get nice extra income, and in turn you help a borrower buy a home who may have been having a hard time.

The point is that there is never an excuse as to why you can't buy a home. If you want to buy a home and you can't, it's only because you aren't willing to try hard enough or take the risk. There are always people out there willing to lend money for a return.

When you have enough properties, you may want to start setting money of your own aside to start buying homes in cash so you don't have to worry about the loan process tying you up. Buying properties in cash will also allow you to buy more distressed and auction homes. Auction homes are homes that have been foreclosed on and the bank is getting rid of the property using a bidding process. This will typically happen at your local courthouse, or sometimes even online.

A foreclosure is when a homeowner stops paying their mortgage and the bank that holds the mortgage takes it back. These banks want to get rid of foreclosures quickly. Most of the time the bank has already made their money ten times over by the borrower so they just want to liquidate the asset and free up more capital to lend out again. This is where huge deals can be found.

Your county should have a website to show these foreclosed properties that are going to auction. This website will show the date and time of the auction as well as pictures and the starting bid of each home. Run the numbers on each property and decide how high you can go and make enough money that you are happy. Homes can be sold for half of what the going rate would be at these auctions. I've seen people buy homes and later make six figure profits by selling it 2 months later. These auctions can provide tons of opportunity to get into a deal. Although, you have to hand over a cashiers check for the full amount of the property when the final bid is done, no financing available here.

Buying foreclosures can be a great way to get distressed homes at a good price, but you need to do your research on the properties first. Make sure you cover all of your bases before you pull the trigger on the property. You need to address a few factors before buying a foreclosure. Are the owners still living in it? Is anyone else squatting in the property? Did they destroy the home knowing it would be going back to the bank? Are there any other liens on the property you need to be aware of? What is the after repair value or ARV? These are all questions you need address.

I have seen foreclosures with homeless people living inside squatting, taking more than 3 month to get them out. I have seen owners pour concrete into the plumbing creating a rehab nightmare. I've seen many disastrous situations, these being among the worst. Foreclosures are a beast of their own, make sure you know what you're getting into before putting all of your hard earned cash into one.

Using your own money to buy rental properties can make things quite a bit simpler, but it can also tie you up financially if you don't have a large surplus of capital. When investing in real estate I like to use as little of my own money as possible. Even billionaires don't sink all of their own capital into a deal. Many super successful people became that way by partnering up and splitting time, effort and profits. It is always better to get loans and leverage your properties than to put your own cash down. Many investors will fight me on this, but let me explain and you can make your own decision.

Just imagine you have been doing real estate for a while and you now have $200,000 in extra cash saved up. Many investors would use this money and pay cash for a $200,000 home. Let me explain to you why leveraging your real estate properties is better than paying cash for them.

You now have $200,000 in the bank. Assuming your properties aren't owner occupied, you have to put a 20% down payment down. The average home price in your area is $200,000. Any good real estate investor likes to abide by the 1% rule. Meaning the rent you can get from the home is a minimum 1% of the purchase price. Let's say this home rents for 1% of the purchase price which is $2,000. You can either purchase 1 home at $200,000 with all of your cash and get $2,000 per month in passive income. Or you can leverage your money. Having to put

20% down on a $200,000 house is $40,000. With $40,000 as a down payment you can purchase five $200,000 homes. $40,000 down payment X 5 homes = $200,000 = what you have in the bank.

You have now put $40,000 down on five $200,000 houses. Leaving your mortgage amount at $160,000. $200,000 purchase price - $40,000 down payment = $160,000 to be financed. The typical mortgage amount on a $160,000 loan at 5% interest over 30 years is roughly $859. With taxes and insurance let's just call it $1,000. Now you have to pay a lender $5,000 every month in mortgages. You purchased five homes with a mortgage of $1,000 on each property equaling $5,000 in mortgages that you owe per month on your five properties. Remember these were $200,000 homes. Assuming you abided by the 1% rule. These homes will be renting for $2,000 each. 5 homes X $2,000 per month = $10,000 per month in income. Don't forget you have to pay your lender $5,000 in mortgages per month on these properties. $10,000 income - $5,000 paid in mortgages = $5,000 in positive cash flow per month.

Let's look back. You had $200,000 in the bank. You could have paid cash for 1 property worth $200,000 and received 1% in rent being $2,000 every month. Or you could have leveraged your properties and purchased five of them with $1,000 positive cash flow each brining in $5,000 in income every month. Paying cash for that property would bring you $240,000 in cash flow in10 years. If you leveraged and bought those five properties instead, you would have brought in $600,000 in 10 years and that is just cash flow not appreciation or loan pay down. These are crucial mistakes people make every day. You can almost triple your income every month when you leverage your money this way. This will add up immensely. This simple mistake could have cost you millions over 30 years. Let me explain why.

The five homes you just purchased are mortgaged over 30 years. After 30 years when your five mortgages are paid off. Your rental portfolio will be worth $1,000,000. Five homes worth

$200,000 each paid off. Once they are paid off and you don't owe your lender any more money you are getting 100% of the cash flow. Meaning you have 5 house at $200,000 bringing in 1% each. That means you are receiving the whole $10,000 every month after paying the mortgages off. You are now making 6 figure income without putting in any work. Every month you have 5 checks for $2,000 each coming in.

To go a step further, after 30 years when you pay these loans off, imagine if you took that $1,000,000 cash and purchased more real estate with it instead of letting it sit. If we use the same numbers; $200,000 house with a $40,000 down payment on each. You would be able to purchase 25 homes now instead making you $25,000 per month. 25 homes bringing $1,000 cash flow per month. You see how powerful and exponential this can be.

Hopefully you haven't forgotten your twin who is now miserable after deciding to buy one house with his $200,000 cash. After 30 years they are still getting just $2,000 cash every month. The home was paid off to begin with. Just to put it in perspective.

Over your 30 year loan term your twin who paid cash for one house made $720,000 in rental income from his $200,000 every month. Not too bad. You on the other hand brought in a whopping $1.8 million. Receiving $5,000 per month in positive cash flow over 30 years. By being smart, knowing the game and how to play it. You made well over double what he made. These choices and this knowledge is what separates the average investors from the high rollers.

Investing in real estate isn't as hard as it sounds. What if you could buy your first property for just $750? You can, here's how it works. Buying a home for this amount of money or even less can be possible with the FHA loan. This is the Federal Housing administration loan, designed to help people buy homes with lower down payments. This loan requires you to have a minimum 3.5% down payment.

For this example we will use a $150,000 house. For a $150,000 house, duplex, triplex or quadraplex you must have a $5,250 down payment. 3.5% of $150,000. You find the property you want to purchase, you talk to your lender and get pre-approved to buy the home. You put your $5,250 down payment in and purchase the home. On the day the money goes through and you've actually purchased the house, you will now get a check for $4,500. Why? Because you followed my first step of real estate investing and got your real estate license. You, as a realtor, just represented yourself on your own home purchase. Your average commission for buying or selling a home is 3% of the selling price. You were required to have a down payment equalling 3.5% of the selling price. This allows you to buy just about any home, for just .5% down.

Yes you must come up with the 3.5% initially, but I'm sure in your sphere of influence you can find someone to loan you that money for a couple of weeks, you're guaranteed to get it back if the home actually sells.

It gets better. Earlier in this book I talked about USDA loans. These are loans the United States Department of Agriculture grants for people willing to buy a property outside of a dense metro area. These loans require 0% down. If you have your real estate license and you found a house to purchase that qualifies for a USDA loan, you could purchase a $250,000 house with $0.00 down. When the house closes and you get the keys, you also get a commission check for $7,000 from the seller for representing yourself in this transaction. That $7,000 is enough to fix up the property, or even do another deal with. I hope you understand how powerful this is. You can buy a home and the seller of that home will pay you $7,000 just for doing some paperwork on your own home purchase and 'representing yourself' as the buyer for the property.

There are many different ways to buy property creatively. All it takes is the knowledge and willingness to execute. Many people learn everything about real estate and never take action. All of these examples are extremely possible, real estate can change you and your families lives forever. You just have to take the initiative and make it happen.

- 6 -

BUY AND HOLD

Real estate is my favorite investment vehicle because of how many different ways you can make money. You have tax benefits, appreciation (economic inflation causes home prices to rise), equity, and cash flow or rental income.

The tax benefits come in when writing off expenses such as mortgage interest, maintenance expenses, property management (paying a company to handle your rental home), depreciation, property tax, and travel expenses. These can be crucial when investing in real estate to maximize profits. With cash flow and other streams of income coming in, you will need to take advantage of every tax deduction you can to maximize the money you take home. It doesn't matter how much you make, it matters how much you keep. Nothing hurts more than having a good year and receiving a big bill from the IRS at the beginning of the year.

Appreciation is the increase in a home's value over time because of improvements, inflation in the economy, or inflation in your market. Appreciation usually happens slowly. It's a nice bonus when buying real estate. You never want to count on appreciation when you buy because it is never guaranteed that your home will naturally raise in value with the market. There are too many factors involved to accurately predict this, just like with any investment. History proves that the housing market is cyclical, fluctuating up and down as time passes.

Equity is the money that is paid every month on your mortgage that is being directly applied to the principle above and beyond the interest you're paying the bank for borrowing their money. Every month this money is slowly applied to your loan which will lower your overall debt. If your 30 year mortgage is $1,000 per month, you will generally pay around $750 in interest and $250 toward your principle in the beginning of the loan term. These numbers slowly switch as the years pass. In the first few years of your loan term, you pay mostly interest and by the end of the loan term, you are paying almost no interest at all.

We already know what cash flow is from the previous chapter, it will be your best friend throughout life. When buying real estate for the long term and getting this cash flow, it is important not to just blow it. Play the long game. If you're spending money as fast as you're making it, you're playing a short game.

Always set some money aside when investing in real estate to account for mortgage insurance, taxes, and capital expenditures. Capital expenditures or "capex" is just a fancy word for maintenance and updating. Capex can be anything from a water heater breaking, to hiring a gardener to landscape every month.

Capex is usually just maintenance on your property. It is extremely important to account for these expenses and set money aside for things like capex when looking at a real estate deal. People get in trouble when they get their extra $700 each month from their first deal and decide to go out and buy a new car with a $700 payment. This is not the way to invest. The key to creating longterm wealth that will last is to be conscious of your spending and don't over-extend yourself.

The best time to start investing is now. Don't wait, you aren't too old, you aren't too young. Just start. Imagine you're 30 years old. Over the next 5 years you devote your time and effort to finding and funding new buy and hold real estate deals. The next 5 years you acquire a nice portfolio of 15 homes worth about $150,000 each. (To many of you, this may seem like an incredible feat, but trust me, this is extremely attainable). The more deals you do, the easier the next one is. The more homes you have, the more money you have coming in to buy your next one. This process will snowball and your portfolio will grow exponentially over time.

Let's say we abide by this 1% rule, and each $150,000 home that you have, rents for $1,500. You probably would have structured your loans over 30 years which is normal. So let's fast forward 30 years. If you didn't buy another rental property over the next 30 years and just kept your portfolio the same at 15 houses. Assuming your mortgages were $800, not only would you have made an extra $700 on top of your payments ($1,500 rent - $800 mortgage = $700 in your pocket for each house). Cash flow alone, over the 30 year period you would make $3.8 million from these houses. $700 per month in cash flow X 15 houses = $10,500. $10,500 in income every month for 30 years is just a hair under $3.8 million.

Let's say your homes would appreciate around 30% over the next 30 years making them worth $195,000 each instead of $150,000. Adding this appreciation to the cash flow rental income, you're now looking at $4,905,000 that you would have made in the last 30 years. Just from buying rental properties. That equates to $13,625 per month or $163,500 per year that you are making by simply being patient.

All you had to do was put in that hard work in the beginning. Without the appreciation, you would be bringing in $10,500 in pure cash flow every month from your 15 home rental portfolio. If you wanted, you could just retire at 35 and live a great life, make a nice six figure income with unlimited free time. This is why real estate is so attractive.

All you need to do is decide on a number. Figure out how much money you would have to make each month to retire and do whatever you want to do. For some people its $3,000 per month and for some it is $300,000. Since we are abiding by this 1% rule where the house price rents for 1% of the homes purchase price. Just do the math. If all you want is $3,000 in income when you retire, you need a $300,000 investment property paid off brining you that 1% each month ($3,000). To determine what you will need if you would like to retire today, you simply have to determine how much cash flow you will need to acquire above your initial mortgage payment. If you need a $3,000 per month passive income stream to replace your current income and each property yields an average cash flow of $300 per month, you'll need 10 properties.

Imagine you're 35 and your 15 property portfolio has allowed you to retire with $10,500 coming in every month. Your friend who is the same age, chooses to work for some big company and is on schedule to retire at 65. Imagine you're both 65 years old now, he retires and finally has the free time to do what he wants.

Meanwhile, you had your 15 homes mortgaged out for 30 years and you stopped investing when you were 35, so your mortgages are now all paid off. With appreciation, your homes are now worth an average of $195,000 accounting for the 30% appreciation over 30 years. While your friend is excited about his pension and 401k. You have a big decision to make. You no longer have your mortgage cutting into your cash flow. Assuming we still abided by the 1% rule. You would have raised your rents to market rents which would be $1,950 for one of your $195,000 homes. This is when it gets exciting. You can either continue to take the monthly cash flow, instead of $10,500 per month, you would bring in $29,250 per month almost tripling your income because these mortgages are paid off. Another option would be to liquidate your entire portfolio, sell everything and cash out. This would bring you a whopping $2.9 million dollars. So what would you choose? Triple your monthly income? Or sell everything and cash out for a lottery-like payday? If you wanted to sell everything you're looking at a paycheck of $2,925,000. It may be hard to resist this. Just think, if you kept the rental income, over the next 8 years of that $29,250 per month rental income, you would make about the same as you would if you sold entirely. Except you still have that portfolio after the 8 years.

I don't want to get into too much real estate fancy footwork, but I am all about creating actual value. I want you to read this book and have real life tools that you can work with. My background is in real estate, I eat, sleep and breathe it. I am going to give you one (of many) ways you can start investing in real estate today.

It's called the **B.R.R.R.R.** strategy. It stands for Buy, Rehab, Rent, Refinance, Repeat. This is my favorite way to acquire properties. The key in this strategy is finding a good home to buy below market value. Imagine you buy a property that is undervalued for $150,000 and you put 20% down, which is $30,000. The property is kind of beat up and all of the other homes similar to it in the area are worth upwards of $200,000. So you buy the home and put another $20,000 into fixing it up and consequently you raise the value in sync with the others in the neighborhood, $200,000. The next step would be to rent the home out. Standing by the 1% rule. You would rent it for $2,000 per month. After you get the renter in there (quickly, so you don't have to keep paying the mortgage yourself). You go to a bank and have them do a cash out refinance.

What the bank would do is get the house appraised. Let's say it is just as nice as the other houses now, maybe a little nicer because of some new things you've added, and it would appraise for $220,000. The bank would give you everything except for 20% or $44,000. When refinancing, a bank will only let you take out a 80/20 LTV or loan to value ratio. Which means you can take 80% of the homes value out of the house in cash.

Let's refresh. You bought the home for $150,000 with $30,00 down. And $20,000 toward improving the home for a total of $50,000 of your cash spent. The original loan was $120,000 (Home price - Downpayment = Loan amount). This home is now worth $220,000. The bank would give you 80% of the appraised value being $176,000. You have to pay your old loan off, that was $120,000 leaving you with $56,000 cash. Initially you put $30,000 down, and $20,000 into construction, to make $50,000 total spent and you just gained $56,000 from the cash out refinance, leaving you all paid back for the money you spent with an extra $6,000. You now have a home with a renter in it, paying your new mortgage and providing you with a steady stream of cash flow every month. You also have a home worth around $220,000 with $0 cash spent and you even made an extra $6,000. Your initial downpayment on the home was $30,000 and your construction costs were $20,000 which you got back after the refinance plus $6,000. After this deal you now have an extra $56,000 to put into the next deal while now owning a cash flowing house basically for free. This process is great because of how much it can snowball. Do this a few times and you can be set for life.

This is why I like real estate investment so much. With stocks, you can't touch them. You can't go to them and make them look more attractive when their price drops a little bit. Real estate is tangible and will always have value. No matter what, people always need a place to live. What if the market crashed and a bunch of people lose their homes? This is when my motto, "Never Sell" comes into play. If you don't over leverage yourself and bite off more than you can chew. Those people who lose their houses will be forced to rent from you some day.

I want to make sure you read this book and can immediately take action. No excuses. Assuming you're going to do step one first (get your real estate license) so your step two needs to be to buy your first home. Buy a home for yourself. Take the initiative and make it happen. Start by finding a lender in your town on google, or talk to other homeowners about who they got their loan from. Your lender will be able to go over everything that you need to buy your first property and their knowledge is free. Call one and schedule your first appointment to get the ball rolling. Think you're too early and can't afford one? Still talk to a lender because they will tell you exactly what you need to do to buy a home. Their job is to get you into a home and trust me, they want to.

For your first home, I recommend looking into a duplex, triplex, or quadraplex because you can do something many people call "house-hacking". House-hacking is when you buy a home and rent it out while you're living in it. Have some friends? Buy a house and rent the other rooms out to your friends to cover the cost of the mortgage. Once you're settled and ready to get your next deal, simply rent your room out and move out. You'll have a full rental property just like that. The reason I like house-hacking larger properties is because it provides more opportunity for cash flow. Generally, the more units you have, the more cash flow you can get. Buy a duplex, live in one side, rent the other side out for the cost of the mortgage and live for free. Even if their side of the duplex doesn't exactly cover the mortgage, I guarantee you'll be paying less every month than you would if you were renting from someone else, and you own the place.

In many areas properties are expensive. Being from California, it gets extremely hard to find deals that cash flow. An average 3/2 house will sell for around $250,000, but may never rent for $2,500. Maybe $1,400 if you're lucky. So I'm forced to get creative. Although there are always deals to be found, they can be few and far between. Instead of taking the time to scrounge for deals at the bottom of the barrel in my local market, I began looking elsewhere. There are many cities that offer good numbers. For instance, I can buy just about the same house I bought in California for $240,000 in Memphis, TN for about $70,000 and also in Little Rock, AR for about the same price. Lower prices mean you can buy more units. The more units you have, the easier you can get to that 1% rule. Here in California could find a quadraplex for around $400,000 and rent the whole thing for around $4,000 total. But single family homes make it tough.

Typically the more units you buy, the better the cash flow. My advice is to go as big as possible as soon as possible. Real estate snowballs, once it gets going, it grows exponentially. When you finally get your first rental property, it will provide you with cash flow, this extra money makes it easier to buy your next deal. When you buy that next deal and you have cash flow coming in from both deals. That makes it twice as easy to buy your next deal after that. Before you know it, you will be snowballing into a large rental portfolio and it just gets easier. This snowball effect can be put into overdrive with multifamily properties. Multifamily properties are basically any property with more than one dwelling. It can be a duplex with two houses connected, or a 100 unit apartment complex.

My advice is to scale up to as many units as you can as early as you can. Large multifamily buildings create many opportunities for income, but buying them can be tricky. Any multifamily property with more than 4 units is considered commercial, not residential. These commercial units cannot be purchased with your standard home loan. You have to get special financing for these apartment buildings. Smaller multifamily buildings can be purchased as an owner occupied residence, which will get you a better break on interest and your terms. Where large multifamily properties can not be purchased using owner occupied terms.

Small multifamily 1-4 unit buildings can be purchased using any FHA, USDA, VA, or conventional financing. Using one of these loan types can save you tons of money on the front end.

Large multifamily properties aren't valued like normal homes. They are valued using something called a "cap rate" which is short for capitalization rate. This rate is shown as a percentage: NOI (net operating income) divided by market value (sales price). This percentage will show you the potential rate of return on this investment.

NOI is the income that the property produces, minus all of the expenses that the property incurs to keep running such as property management, insurance, property tax, repairs, and maintenance. A years worth of NOI is added up, and divided by the current sales price to give you your cap rate. Cap rates aren't like sales prices where you can instantly look at the number and tell if the property is a good deal or not. You really have to understand the area in which you are buying to decide if the cap rate will work for you. For instance, a 3% cap rate in San Francisco, CA would be a good deal, but a horrible deal in Springfield, Missouri. In Montgomery, Alabama a cap rate of 10%

is considered good. Know your deals, know your location and know your numbers.

The only thing cap rate doesn't account for is a mortgage, cap rate only really applies to properties that are paid for in cash. With debt on the property, that will decrease your NOI by quite a bit. For those of you who are aiming to buy a property with financing, there is a more important number to look at. That is your DSCR (debt service coverage ratio).

Your debt service ratio generally needs to be no lower than 1.25x. This (x) simply means times, your NOI covers your debt service 1.25 times. Generally anything above 1x will indicate you should be able to cover your debt comfortably, but we aren't in the game to be comfortable, we want to make money. So I like to see this more around 1.6x. There will always be a rise in vacancy rates and unforeseen instances, so it's good to make sure you have some wiggle room in there.

When purchasing, a large multifamily, you need to have your NOI greater than you overall debt. If you have $20,000 in income per year from your property and your paying $25,000 per

year between your mortgage, insurance, maintenance fees,

property management and so on. You're going to be upside down.

Your DSCR = NOI / annual debt (costs of everything to keep

your property afloat). Calculating your DSCR is the best way to

value a property with a mortgage on it. Let's look at an example.

You're considering buying an apartment complex for $200,000.

The NOI (income) is $30,000, but you financed it and your

mortgage (debt service) is $1,200 per month or $14,400 per year.

You take your NOI for a year, $30,000 and divide it by your debt

service each year $14,400. This gives you 2.08x. Your NOI covers

your debt service 2.08 times. This would be considered a good

investment. You will not be losing money if everything goes

according to plan.

There are many great ways to find value in apartment

complexes. One of the easiest being separate meters for each unit.

Many apartment investors get billed for the water and electricity

use for the entire building. This in my opinion is a huge mistake

Let's say you own a 20 unit apartment building and each unit rents for $1,000 per month. You're binging in $20,000 per month, but you're paying for the water and electricity use of the tenants because it's much simpler that way, you just raised rent a little bit to offset it.

Imagine if you billed that back to the tenants. You can either get a separate meter for each unit which can cost a bit to do, but it's nice when the tenant gets the bill directly and you don't have to deal with it. Or you can pool the usage together and bill back the tenants for an average usage. For example if you acquired a new apartment building and the utility bill for the entire complex was $3,000 per month, you would divide $3,000 by 20 units and bill each tenant for that amount, $150 per unit. Doesn't seem too bad to have tenants pay for their own usage does it?

Making this simple change can make an investor a lot of money. Billing this back to the tenant makes the investor another $3,000 per month. Let's look at this in the macro. An extra $3,000 per month would yield $1,080,000 over a 30 year loan term, assuming you had a mortgage on the property. This is nothing to brush off. To know that so many investors aren't doing this is crazy to me. I understand it looks attractive to potential tenants when the water, sewer, garbage and electricity are "Free", but when a new owner comes in, tenants expect change anyway. So keeping these rents at market and billing them back never rocks the boat too badly.

Change of any kind will always make some tenants leave. That's just business. While you're making different changes after acquiring a new property it's important to learn who your tenants are and understand their needs. It can be a great idea to send a survey out to them to better understand what's most important to them. Maybe it is a park, on site maintenance, accessibility or safety. No matter what it is, listen to their wants and do all you can to create an environment they want to stay in. If they have to pay their own bills each month at an extra $150. Make them feel good about where they live and hire a landscaper to clean up the area and plant flowers. Pressure wash the walkways and respond to their maintenance requests promptly. As long as they feel like they are being heard and you are doing something positive to their environment, they will respect you and stay in your property.

This is just one example of how to add value to a property, there are plenty of different ways to strengthen your real estate investment you just have to know how and when to use them.

The purchase of one decent sized apartment building can set you up for the rest of your life. When I was 19 years old I met a man on a running trail near my house, we ended up chatting and in our conversation he mentioned he was going to Colorado for a week to ski, then to Hawaii to surf and was thinking about going to Paris because he had never been. I was very curious as to what he could've possible done for a living that would give him that time and money. I thought he must have won the lottery or something. After all, I was serving coffee and couldn't even image a life close to that. He told me he owned an apartment complex in Santa Cruz, CA. Yes, just one. I asked him how he got into real estate. He told me a story about him as a teenager. He said that he had just graduated high school and didn't want to go to college. His dad wasn't pleased by the idea and was going to force him to go. His dad said that if he could make $100,000 in the next year, he didn't have to go to college. If he couldn't make $100,000, he was going to college and moving out of his parents house.

Rewind to 1985 he didn't have a job or a car. All he had was an idea for a knock off Disney t-shirt to work with. After borrowing $100 from his dad, he bought ad space in MAD magazine to try and sell these shirts. After the first magazine shipped, he had more orders than he knew what to do with. People were buying his shirts left and right. In that next year he made over $100,000 in profit from those t-shirt sales.

His dad held to his promise and didn't make him go to college, but he wasn't going to let him blow that money on something stupid. This man and his dad devised a plan to use that money to buy an apartment building in Santa Cruz, CA. After searching, they put $100,000 down and bought one in 1987. Day one he said this property was bringing them over $4,000 per month. That's good money in 1987. His property was now paid off and was yielding him an average of $48,000 per month. This absolutely blew my mind. I couldn't fathom making that kind of money, not only making that kind of money, but not having to work for it. He had processes and systems in place so that he didn't have to lift a finger. He was making $576,000 per year by doing nothing. He inspired me to get into real estate and create a life that would allow me to do whatever I want, whenever I want.

Apartments can be a large undertaking, but very rewarding. The more units you have, the more opportunity you have for growth and profit. My philosophy is to scale up as fast as you can, I believe in large multi-family properties. I have seen them make many people a lot of money.

You may be overwhelmed by the numbers in this chapter and think that the examples that I made up are impossible and only happen to those who are super lucky. It isn't as hard as it seems. Being a real estate agent, I see things like this happen all the time. With a little knowledge and the motivation, you can become extremely successful. I'm sure at some point you've asked yourself "If it's so easy, why isn't everyone doing it?" I think you would be surprised by the amount of people who aren't willing to put in the time, work, and take the risks.

To be successful in real estate you have to be a future thinker. If you need instant gratification you will lose in this game. Real estate is for the person who cares about the financial foundation they will lay for generations to come. Real estate may not make you rich as fast as a lottery ticket, but if you're persistent and put the effort in, it can easily give you the life a lottery ticket would. You have to break down that wall of fear blocking you from stepping out of your comfort zone. You don't become successful by staying in the pocket and working your 9-5 day job. You have to take those risks and put the action out there to get the results you desire. Nothing comes easy, but you have to be willing to do what most people won't, to live your life like most people can't.

- 7 -

FIND THE DEALS

Now that you know how the real estate investment world works, you can prepare yourself to purchase your first deal. Finding good deals can be tough because of so many people wanting to get into the real estate game. You really have to get creative and work hard to find these properties that will create the future you desire.

Most deals are found off the market. This means nobody is selling them yet. They aren't on zillow.com, loopnet.com, or even the MLS. These are deals that you find from a friend or you create yourself. Many good deals are found simply by finding a property you'd like to buy, finding the owner, and calling them or sending them a letter about why you want to buy their home.

A good way to find these deals can be as simple as getting in the car and looking for houses that have grass that hasn't been mowed in a long time, it looks like nobody has lived there in a long time, or the people that live there don't take care of it. These might be renters and the landlord might be tired of them and want to just sell the home instead of dealing with them. Drive around and write these addresses down. Take 10 or 15 addressees, find the owners information online or at the county assessors office and contact them. There are many resources online to access this information, some you have to pay a little bit, but it's worth it.

Send them a letter or call them and tell them why you want to buy their home and why they should sell it. Do your due diligence and find the right price for this house and make that offer. If they refuse, move on to the next one, but keep their information and contact them once every few months. At some point I bet they will cave in and get rid of their headache property.

When looking for deals, just remember that every house has a price. Every single piece of property on planet earth has a price that will make sense for an investment. You just have to get it to that price. If you're searching for deals on Zillow or Realtor, ignore the selling price. It doesn't matter a bit what someone thinks their house is worth. The only thing that matters is the number you have to buy it at to make money. Many people will go out and buy a piece of property $20,000 under the asking price and think they got a good deal. This does not mean you got a good deal, this just means you got it $20,000 lower than what the seller wanted to get out of it. Ignore the selling price and know your numbers. I can't emphasize this enough. Know the numbers you need to make money.

Take some time and analyze deals. The more deals you analyze, the more comfortable you will be with the numbers that you need. After analyzing quite a few, you will pretty much be able to look at a house and see if it will cash flow, or work for you pretty easily. By knowing the square footage, bedroom and bathroom count, size of the lot, condition of the house and location, you should be able to look at these numbers and know instantly what you need to buy it for to make money.

If you can't find good deals, make good deals. Take that 2/2 house and add a bedroom. Build an apartment on top of the garage. Negotiate the terms of the deal. Whatever it takes to have the deal make sense for you. You will have to get creative in the real estate world. It may not be as simple as finding a house that is $50,000 under priced, buying it, and taking that $50,000 out in cash. You will have to be flexible and find a way to make some deals profitable. Some deals and sellers just don't want to work. Don't push too hard if things aren't coming together. You have to know when to keep pushing, or move on to the next one. Don't waste too much time on stubborn sellers or disaster properties.

Now that you know the difference between properties and know how to evaluate each one. It's time to make an offer.

Before you make an offer on any property. Make sure you are making the offer based on the property and numbers, not emotion. People often buy out of emotion, they love the vibe of the home or the floor plan and can't live without it. This will get you in trouble quickly. Find the number that makes sense and offer that number. The fastest way to lose money is to buy with your heart instead of your head. Be smart and make only calculated offers that you understand the terms of. Making a bad decision on the buy could cripple you in the long term.

Knowing this will help you immensely while buying and selling real estate. Although you don't want to buy with emotion, most people do. People buy with emotion and justify with logic. When selling a home, you aren't selling the house you're selling the buyers future. Remember this and use this to your advantage when selling homes and submitting offers.

The great thing about having your real estate license is that you can submit as many offers as you want. You don't have to pester another agent to write lower offers on properties and waste anyones time. You can submit an offer on any property in your area at any time. You will get rejected on some, but you have to try. I've seen some extremely low offers get accepted, you never know what kind of position a seller is in. It never hurts to ask. After all, there are good deals to be had everywhere you just need to find them.

When submitting an offer, real estate agent or not, make sure you have a minimum 17 day inspection period in the contract. This will protect you and allow you to back out of the contract you find something about the house that you don't like. After this 17 day inspection period is over, if you want to back out, you will lose your earnest money deposit. An earnest money deposit is a deposit you put into escrow that essentially tells the seller that you're serious about buying the home and are willing to put a bit of money up front for it. Many buyers like to put large deposits down to show the seller they are very serious about buying the home. I never recommend a deposit over $10,000 because this is the most you can get back in small claims court if things turn south.

Getting offers accepted can be tough, but I have a few tricks to make things fall in your favor. One thing to do when submitting an offer to purchase a property is to submit two offers. Both with different terms. This will force the seller to psychologically have to choose between the best of the two offers you gave them, instead of choosing between your offer and someone else's. This really gets the sellers to think, they now have two options to sell their home and this makes them feel like they are in control of the situation. They make the choice that best suits them, and everyone wins.

When looking for a good deal and getting the right price for a property you will make lots of offers and many will get declined. It's a pain to go out and look at every property, run the numbers and make an offer. Instead, since every property has a price that makes sense from an investment standpoint, simply find that price and write an offer for that price. All you have to do is put in the contract "subject to interior inspection". This means that you have not yet been inside the home and are making your offer based on what you believe the property to look like. Once your offer is accepted, you can go to the home and ensure it is truly what the pictures show and it is what you expected it to be. This protects you and allows you to back out of the offer if the property isn't quite what it seems. Many photographers know how to make a dump look good, so be weary.

Another trick I use to quickly evaluate a property is to determine if the house is currently listed at market value and offer 20% less than that. This works best in parallel to the B.R.R.R.R. (buy, rehab, rent, refinance, repeat) method. In this B.R.R.R.R. method you need to have at least 20% equity to pull your money out. Well if you find a property that is at market value and get that home for 20% less, you automatically have 20% equity.

If I see a house for sale for $200,000 and I believe that is an average price, I would offer them $160,000, 20% less than asking. Assuming they accept the offer, this home would cost me

$32,000 initially for the down payment. 20% of $160,000. While in escrow this house appraises for $200,000, market value. At this point I owe $128,000 on a home worth $200,000, $160,000 purchase price minus my $32,000 down payment.

After the home closes you may need to season the loan, some banks won't let you refinance a home until you've paid on the original loan for a period of time anywhere from 1-12 months, this is considered seasoning a loan. After the loan is seasoned, if that's what your new lender requires, you will need to do a cash out refinance. This cash out refinance will allow you to pull out every dollar except 20%. If the house appraises for $200,000 the lender will give you $160,000 cash. You just need to pay your old loan off of $128,000 keeping the difference $32,000. You just bought a home for $0. Your initial investment was $32,000 and you pulled $32,000 out of it.

After doing this and getting your initial investment back you can move on to the next and do this over and over again. All you need is this initial 20% down payment, using this method you could buy an infinite amount of properties. Every time you bought a property you would later get your money back. Your only constraint is time and getting those offers accepted. You need to understand how powerful this is. Look at the average home price in your area and save up 20% of that. You can recycle this money into property after property growing your portfolio exponentially.

Using this method, every dollar that comes to you by renting this property is pure profit because you don't have any money into it, all you have into the deal is time. This is a return any investor would die for. Most investors are happy with their 6% return not even knowing the hundred other ways to make their money work for them. If you are committed to these methods and want it bad enough, your potential can be unlimited.

In real estate, your cash on cash return is one of the most important metrics to determine if a deal is going to be rewarding or not. This is the return you are getting based on the cash you put into your property. To calculate the cash on cash return you look at the true cash flow this property is bringing you each year, after all expenses are paid like PITI (monthly principle payment, interest, taxes and insurance) let's say this property is brining you $200 every month. Let's also say the property costs you $20,000 out of pocket to purchase. To calculate your cash on cash return you simply divide your initial investment by your total pre-tax cash flow for one year. If one years cash flow was $2,400 you would divide this by your $20,000 out of pocket cash to purchase the property equaling 12%. This is a great return for cash on cash.

A nice rule of thumb I try to abide by is to get $100 per month for every $10,000 cash I have invested. This will keep your cash on cash return around that 12% mark. You should be flexible on this given the market and potential appreciation you can receive as well. 12% is considered great, with the average being around 8% for investors. Don't be afraid to take a smaller cash on cash return to buy a property with good projected appreciation and long term tenants. Keeping a property that cash flows for a long period of time will compound your return in the form of appreciation, tax benefits and equity, the longer you keep it, the sweeter the deal gets.

If you are new to real estate investment and are having a hard time analyzing deals, don't worry. Find someone who is experienced and run the deal by them, use them as a resource. It's good to have another person on your side for a second opinion regardless if you are a seasoned investor or brand new to the business.

Never underestimate the value of a partner. To invest in real estate you either have to have time and knowledge, or money. If you have time and knowledge, partner with someone who has money and can buy the deals, while you can find them and coordinate the flip/rental. If you have the money, find someone who has the knowledge and time to find those good deals and can deal with the nuts and bolts of acquiring the property. 50% of a deal, is far better than no deal.

Many investors do something called syndication. This basically means to pool money together to buy a deal you would not normally be able to purchase on your own. Although this sounds like something you'd do if you didn't have a lot of capital, it isn't. Many high net worth investors still don't use all of their own money in a deal. They pool their money together and buy large investments, with each partner drawing dividends from the profit.

There are many different ways to structure syndication deals it depends entirely on your wants and needs. When syndicating there are 2 different types of partners, GP's or general partners and LP's or limited partners. General partners are usually much more involved, they assume most of the risk, structure the deal and manage the asset. This person is in the drivers seat. Limited partners have limited risk involved and are much more passive. As you can tell, the GP usually brings the time and knowledge and the LP usually brings the money.

Since LP's typically bring most of the capital, they should be structured to get their investment back first. Always pay your LP before you pay yourself. Another word of advice when syndicating is to never take anyones money if they can't afford to lose it. There is nothing worse than taking $50,000 from a friend who has a $60,000 net worth. They will call you every day asking about their investment and ask when they are going to start getting paid. Instead of acquiring deals, you'll be babysitting their capital. Before entering into an agreement with anyone, make sure they understand exactly what you are doing and why. This is not a get rich quick situation. Real estate takes time.

Syndications are run like businesses and there are fees involved, such as an acquisition and management fee. A management fee is the fee the sponsor gets for managing the asset and the team involved. Being the one coordinating the syndication you are called a sponsor. As the sponsor it is your job to find these deals and bring people together to invest. The sponsor will usually get an acquisition fee anywhere from 0 to 4 points. These points will help pay for operating costs, property viewing and all the time and effort it takes to acquire a deal. On the short side, many investors get fixed on closing the deal for the acquisition fee. These fees can become enormous when buying large deals. Some sponsors will only focus on closing a deal, they won't worry about how good the deal is because the larger the deal the larger the acquisition fee. Imagine you are acquiring an $8m deal with a 4 point acquisition fee. That's $320,000 you are getting for finding this deal. These numbers can easily distract someone from the goal of finding a good deal and have them looking for any deal to close on.

Like any avenue of real estate, you need to do your research before making any decisions. Syndication can be incredibly rewarding, but holds many different legal obligations. You are handling other peoples money, it should not be taken lightly. Syndication should be treated as a business. Ensure you and your partners have aligned your goals and everyone has a clear understanding of the process and profits involved. You need to have a clear and concise contract drawn up before entering into a transaction. Lines get blurred and many things can get convoluted when investing with anyone. Take the right steps and make sure you and your partners truly understand what you're getting into before acquiring a deal of any size.

- 8 -

WHERE TO INVEST

With all of this information given to you, you may still be thinking about how hard it is to purchase a home in your area. In large cities, the west coast, and east coast, real estate is expensive. In some areas it's near impossible to find a home worth living in for under $800,000. Don't let this stop you. Living in California myself, I thought it was going to be tough to find something reasonably priced to start my investing career. Until I stumbled upon out of state investing. This is exactly what it sounds like. If prices are too high for your liking in your market. Find a market that is more attractive to you.

Many people will tell you to never buy an investment property more than 20 miles away from where you live. If something goes wrong what will you do? If a pipe breaks, or the roof collapses what will you do? These arguments are only for the people who invest fearfully. If you don't feel comfortable investing in something or some place, don't. Simple as that. If you're going to invest, you must be confident. Thankfully, I'm here to instill that confidence and knowledge in you so that you can put this book down and take action in whatever direction you want.

Many people that tell you not to do something are only saying that because they want to protect you from harm, or risk of losing money. Thank them for their concern, and keep pushing forward. Never invest without knowledge. Knowledge is power in this game. The only person who can tell you not to invest in real estate out of your area, would be someone who has done it many times before and I guarantee that person who has done it many times before would never tell you not to. Because I bet they are successful.

California in general is incredibly hard to get this 1% rule. Even when you do find a property that will rent for 1% odds are it is expensive. If this is truly an investment property you have to put 20% down. Well, 20% of a $250,000 property is $50,000. That can be a lot of money for someone to put on the line, especially in the beginning. Here's how to get around this.

Many markets in the U.S. have 3/2 SFR's (3 bedroom/ 2 bathroom Single Family Rentals) for $50,000 - 70,000. Such as Little Rock, AR and Memphis, TN. There are tons of cities that offer more affordable housing. Finding homes that work with the 1% rule are much easier to find in these areas. A nice 3/2 SFR in Memphis, TN can be $65,000 and can generally rent for around $700.

Since it's an investment property you're buying, you have to put down a 20% down payment. 20% of this property in

Memphis is only $13,000 VS. the property in California which requires $50,000 down and doesn't even abide by the 1% rule and probably won't cash flow a dollar.

Great, now you know that homes can easily be found that abide by the 1% rule and aren't super expensive, but they're out of your area. How would you do that? Out of state investing isn't as hard as it sounds or some people make it sound.

Your first step in out of state investing is to find your market. Do your research, then do it again. Out of state investing only works if you understand the out of state market just as good as you understand your current market. Why not invest in Jacksonville, FL if you understand the Jacksonville market more than you understand your own?

Someone who is agains this idea will usually have only one argument. This is; what if something goes wrong, and you're not there to fix it. The whole point of investing in real estate is to create a passive income stream. If this persons property has a problem and they are the only one to fix it, they're doing it wrong in the first place. Buy your deals to account for this. You don't want to buy rental properties to have freedom and be stuck fixing them all the time. This simply comes down to buying the property right to account for these expenses and you won't have to worry about them.

There is someone out there in every town whose job it is to fix any problem that could happen with your property. Have a house in Kentucky and the roof collapses? There's a roof company to fix that. Hot water heater goes out? Handymen are there to fix that. Tenants move out and trash the place? Property manager is there to fix that.

Many investors search for the right deal, then try and find an agent, lender, property manager, and sometimes a contractor if work needs to be done. This is wrong. After finding your market, step two is to find and build your team. For example let's say you have chosen Alexander, VA as the market you want to invest in. The next step is to find a lender in that area. Go online and read reviews for Alexander lenders and find one who has a good record. Call them up and find out what real estate agent they recommend. Call that real estate agent. While you're on the phone, ask them what they think of the lender you called initially just for some validation. While you're talking to the agent, ask them about a property manager they recommend. Call that property manager, and ask them about the agent and the lender. If everything checks out, ask the property manager for their recommendation for a contractor.

This is an easy way to build a team out of state. Have this real estate agent send you good deals when they come across to them. If the agent sends you a house and says it will rent for $1,000 per month, call your property manager and ask them how much the house would rent for. Next go to rentometer.com to see what that shows. If the numbers are far off from each other, you have a problem and may need to find a different team member. The whole point of this is to create checks and balances within your team to make sure everyone is truly working for your best interests and not theirs.

Once you feel you've connected with a good team. Spend the few hundred dollars and fly into that city and meet each one of your team members. Meet with your lender and talk about current rates and their favorite areas in the city. Have your agent take you to their favorite neighborhoods and favorite places to invest (it's best to find an agent that invests themselves so they truly have an understanding of the world). Go over current rents with your property manager and talk about where they think the market is going. Finally, meet with your contractor at a job site, talk with him about his rehabs and the overall condition of the market. See how well he works with his team.

It takes a lot of trust from you to put your money into these peoples hands, but you need to understand that their job depends on them being successful just like you. Your lender gets paid when you get a loan through them. When you buy a home, your agent gets paid. When your house rents, your property manger makes money. When you fix things at your property, your contractor gets paid. Make sure these individuals know that you plan on doing multiple deals. They know that they need to keep you happy to keep the deals coming in. When you set this expectation, your property manager won't want to fail because they know that if they do, you will pull all of your properties from them and give your business to their competitor.

Out of state rentals can be one of the best ways to invest in real estate. If you replace fear with knowledge you will have no problem. Investing out of state is no different from investing in your current location, if the toilet breaks in a rental that's next to your house you shouldn't want to fix that anyway. Let someone else fix that while you're focusing on doing more deals. Same goes if the toilet breaks in a house 1,000 miles away. You will still hire someone to fix it. If you want to fix toilets and are really good at it, perhaps you should be a plumber. If you are really low on capital and you need to DIY some of the repairs of course that isn't the end of the world, but if you are low on capital, you may have bought a bad deal in the first place. You should always leave room in your analysis for capex (unforeseen issues that may need fixing). This will eliminate the need to ever fix anything yourself.

You should have laser focus on the things that truly make you money, finding deals and building relationships that will get you deals.

There are many ways to invest in out of state rental properties. If you have less time and more money, you may want to consider a 'turn-key' company. One that can do all of the relationship building for you and simply find you deals for you to buy and not think about. I am personally agains turn-key companies because I believe they tend to take advantage of you. In turn-key, there is a lot of profit made by the company before it gets to you. When you buy a property from a turn-key company they take care of a lot of the hassle with rehabbing the house, but you also get charged full market value for it, in some cases, more. It's always better to put the time in and build the deals yourself to generate income on the buy side, the flip side and the rent side. With turn-key, you're only making money on the rent side.

The basis behind turn-key companies is to buy a dilapidated home, fix it up, rent it out, and sell it with the renter inside. Luckily these companies typically obey by the 1% rule as well. This means that from my home in California I can buy a newly renovated house in Jacksonville, FL with a renter inside, renting at 1% of the purchase price and cash flow instantly.

Turn-key companies can be valuable because the company will usually have agents, lenders, contractors, and property managers in house. This creates a nice fluid experience. They gather the entire team that it takes to buy, rehab and rent the property. Another valuable aspect of buying a turn-key home is that their personal contractor will perform the rehab, so you can usually bet that they are going to do a good job. If they don't, their property manager is going to have to deal with the repercussions of having a subpar rehab and they won't want to deal with that headache. So you can usually count on quality construction with these turn-key properties.

This same positive can also be a negative. Since they are all so interconnected, they can work together to hide certain things and inflate certain numbers. This can be very dangerous. If you're interested in buying a turn-key home, there are many companies available, but please do your due diligence and ensure they are a legitimate operation. Fly out to see your property and look at the renovation yourself. Never take anyones word for it. Run the numbers and do everything yourself before pulling the trigger.

Turn-key companies have become semi-famous for inflating numbers. They post a house for sale for $50,000 and it rents for $1,000/mo. You buy the deal because you can't believe it. There have been instances where companies have put a fake renter in the unit for a couple of months until you buy the property, then they "move out" and you can barely get $500 in rent for your junky house.

Always do the numbers yourself. It doesn't matter what anyone tells you. Crunch every number yourself and make sure it works for your investing criteria before taking a step forward in any deal.

Turn-key companies can be a very good way for someone to invest if they don't have a lot of time. Although you will pay more if you go through a turn-key company than you would if you purchased the house, fixed it up, and rented it out yourself. You are essentially paying for the luxury of having someone do all that work for you, just know, you're paying for it.

Investing can be scary. There are many unknowns. The only thing that is for sure, is that the biggest mistake you can make is not investing. You have to be in the game to get the benefits. This can get risky and requires patience and discipline. Once you're in it, I guarantee you'll never leave. The only thing that can eliminate some of this fear, is knowledge. If you have all of the knowledge to invest, you will be able to invest confidently and jump over any hurdles that come your way.

- 9 -

TAKE ACTION

It is time to overcome that fear holding you back from doing what you dream of. Buying real estate can be extremely nerve-wracking. These are huge investments, life changing moves. There are many irrational fears about investing in real estate and I want you to overcome those. Everyone will tell you to stay out of debt, your family, friends, everybody. This is naive. There is good debt and bad debt. Good debt is generally anything under 5% interest. A car loan, or mortgage. Things that are necessary to survive. Bad debt is above that 5% mark such as credit cards and high interest personal loans. These need to go first.

When buying properties many people will tell you to only pay cash, that mortgages are risky. This couldn't be more false. I have gone over a few examples with you already, but this is so important for your future I am going to go over it again. If you had $100,000 cash and we were abiding by the 1% rule. You could buy one property for $100,000 that would bring you $1,000 per month and that's it, maybe a little appreciation if you're lucky. You could take that same $100,000 and get mortgages, if you had to put 20% down on each property, you would be able to purchase 5 homes worth $100,000. 20% X $100,000= $20,000. $20,000 X 5 properties= Your initial holding of $100,000. Now that you have purchased 5 properties.

Let's take a look at your income. Each property is bringing in $1,000 per month. That means that 5 properties would bring you to $5,000 in income every month. Your mortgage for $80,000 ($100,000 purchase price- $20,000 down payment=

$80,000) would be around $650 per month. 5 properties with a $650 mortgage on each one would be $3,250 per month. This means that you have $5,000 coming in, and $3,250 going out every month. Leaving you with $1,750 in profit each month where if you paid cash for your $100,000 property you would only be bringing in $1,000. Just by leveraging (mortgaging your properties) you've increased your income every month by $750. This is just cash flow. That appreciation that you would get on your one property, you would also get on your now 5 properties. You would get 5 times the appreciation that you would if you just bought one property and paid cash. That $1,750 in profit every month doesn't even account for the equity you're getting in each property. Over a 30 year mortgage you would be averaging roughly around $300 per month in equity for every property that someone else is paying as well. So in reality you only see $1,750 in your pocket, but you're getting an extra $1,500 every month in equity. Let's just say you had 30 year mortgages on each property and for simplicity, the properties didn't appreciate at all. In 30 years when those mortgages are paid off. You would have 5 properties each worth $100,000. That's $500,000. In that same 30 years, the property you paid cash for is still just worth $100,000.

It's easy to talk about, and hard to do. I owe every bit of success and happiness in my life to overcoming the fears that I have had. Once you learn how to set fear aside, you will truly be able to see what the best things in life are all about.

The best positions I have ever been in in my life have been right after I've taken a big risk. Fear is only a mindset that needs to be conquered. Change what fear means to you and you will unlock the ability to thrive.

Acting in fear and panic will lose you more money than any market or natural disaster in the world. Your mind will constantly fight against you to be safe because of how it's been conditioned. Many of the most successful people make fast and precise decisions. Think about a time when you were really scared. How did you handle the situation? How should you have handled the situation? I can remember a time when I was younger. Me and some friends drove a few hours up to some cliffs we heard about. We watched videos of people jumping off these cliffs into the water below and thought it looked fun so we decided to try it. After a long car ride we arrived, the cliffs were huge. Upwards of 80 feet high into a creek that looked 5 feet deep. Completely petrified I tried to keep my cool as my friends made the ascent to the top of the cliff.

We finally made it to the top. I thought the cliffs looked high from the bottom, when I glanced over the edge, I could see the end of my life at the bottom. Everyone was hyped up, I knew I had to jump. One of my friends glances over the edge, backs up and runs at it full force throwing his body into a backflip. He jumped out of the water without a scratch. The rest of my friends jumped quickly after, leaving me alone at the top staring down. This was quite possibly the most scared I've ever been. I stared at the bottom until my mind completely melted. My mind wouldn't let me jump, this was the exact opposite of everything we've been taught as young kids. After getting heckled by my friends enough, I jumped (thanks friends).

I went against every single thing my mind is told to do. If your friends jumped off a cliff would you? I just did. Flying through the air hurling towards the water I couldn't help but think how stupid it was. Best case scenario I jump in water worst case scenario I die. The risk/ reward analysis didn't quite add up. I could've stood at the bottom and jumped in the water. After all, I would end up in the same water.

After flying through the air for what seemed like 30 minutes, I finally hit the water. After taking a quick inventory of myself, checking vitals, making sure I still had my eyeballs, arms and swim shorts, I was relieved. I realized It was one of the craziest most fun things I've ever done. After I jumped, we all ran to the top to jump again and again. This has taught me that after you set fear aside and jump into something, it isn't all that bad and you're able to do it many more times without faltering. You almost always come out the other end realizing the thing you were so afraid really isn't that bad, it just took the leap of faith of actually doing it to figure that out.

The same thing will happen to you after you buy your first property. You will be nervous, anxious maybe a little scared, but after the deal is done I guarantee you will laugh at your prior feelings and do whatever it takes to buy another.

This shows how sometimes, within reason, you have to just make a quick precise decision. Overthinking will only make the fear inflate and eat you alive. My mother has always told me everything that will happen to me in life will either be a lesson or a blessing. It just depends on how you look at it. While flying through the journey to success you may have doubts, but in the end, you'll be glad you did it and I bet you will want to do it again.

Decisions should always be calculated, but executed quickly and precisely. You often have to be ahead of your mind and beat it to the punch of false fear. To live the life you've always dreamed of, it doesn't start with money, it starts within yourself and in your mind. When you make a conscious effort to change the way you think and act on a daily basis, you will create the

foundation that will allow you to be successful and prosper in

anything you do. One of my favorite quotes is from Dr. Wayne

Dyer, it goes "When you change the way you look at things, the

things you look at will change" never forget this.

I now have this question for you; who are you going to

be? Our actions are what define us, not our words, so go out there

and make it happen, prove to the world you deserve more from

life. Stop putting it off and make that choice to start investing. On

your deathbed, you are not going to say 'someday i will' and I

guarantee that day, you'll regret saying it now.

Being an entrepreneur isn't for everyone. I whole

heartedly believe you are born with it. Anyone can open a

business, but it takes a specific person to make it something great.

The reason an entrepreneur is successful is because they believe in

themselves and are willing to work harder than every single other

person out there. At times the path of a real estate investor may

hold uncertainty, but it's important to stay focused on the future and what it holds, not the possibility of failure. If you fully commit to your vision and don't make failure an option, you will succeed.

Fearing failure will be one of the hardest things for you to get over. You only fail if you give up. You will never win everything in life or in business. There will be wins and there will be losses almost every day. Nearly every business on the planet has almost failed. They succeeded only because they never gave up and believed in themselves.

Most large businesses have had major failures, some bad enough that they almost had to shut their doors. A few years into business, CLIFF bar made a bad deal with one of their suppliers and got sued for ownership of the company. Gary Erickson, owner of CLIFF bar could have lost everything if he had given up, but he didn't. He fought until the end and won his company back by the skin of his teeth. Gary went from making granola bars in his mothers kitchen for his friends to being worth over $850 million.

Instagram started as a location sharing app called 'Burbn'. After a short time they realized the app was going nowhere and had to create something different. They figured out their users liked the photo feature on their location app most. So instead of giving up, they doubled down on their strength, being photos, and created what we now know to be Instagram, valued at over 35 billion.

Airbnb was floating their entire business on a baseball card binder full of credit cards after no investor would touch them. They got in contact with 20 investors from Silicon Valley, 10 of those investors replied to their emails, 5 of them met to hear more about their business plan and 0 of them invested. Owners Joe Gebbia and Brian Chesky thought it was all over when their credit card debt was drowning them at over $25,000. They resorted to selling bootleg cereal boxes with Obama's face on them for money (seriously). They thought it was over. Joe and Brian soon got connected with the leader of an incubator program to help startup companies. They got the opportunity to interview with the leader Paul Graham. They absolutely bombed the interview and the investor denied them. Feeling defeated, Joe Gebbia gave a box of their Obama themed cereal to Paul as a thank you gift for his time. They told Paul a 60 second story behind the cereal and left. A few moments later on their drive home they received a phone call from Paul. Paul was astonished by the amount of grit and perseverance these two showed by making an effort to get their company out of debt by selling cereal. He put them into the program which jump-started Airbnb into what it is now, valued at over 35 billion dollars.

The biggest triumphs come right after the biggest difficulties. Just when you've hit rock bottom, you have nowhere to go but up.

99% of what fear really is, is fear of judgment. You're afraid of what people will say when you have to live in a smaller house for a while to put money into your business. You're afraid of what people will think when you drive around your old beat up car with a mountain of credit card debt because you're putting every dollar toward your dream.

You only want to share your dreams with the people that will be excited, energetic, and support you on your journey. I'm sure you can already think of a friend or two who are die hard and will tell you to follow your dreams no matter what. They want you to do what makes you happy. These are the people that you need to surround yourself with.

It is important no matter what path you take in life is to stay true to yourself. Life will throw many choices at you. Make every decision confidently and no matter what happens, live life with no regrets. There have been many studies done on the regrets of the dying. People and publications set out on a mission to find out what people regret most on their deathbed, when the person knew there was little time left. Time and time again, study after study, each result is near the same. Almost every single dying individual regrets not what they did do, but what they didn't do. This means after their life is almost over, they didn't take back a single thing that they did do, but they wish they would've taken that risk and done what they were too afraid to do.

People make excuses for everything, I don't have time, I don't have money. This all breaks down to the fact that they are too afraid to pull the trigger on their big dreams or ideas. Yes, investing in real estate can be nerve-wracking. There can be a lot of money involved and this is an asset class with a lot of moving parts. You just need enough knowledge to play defense if a mistake is made, and play offense when the time is right. Work hard to gain that knowledge. If you work 40 hours every week, that leaves 128 hours on the table to work on your passion. I realize everyone needs to sleep and have a work life balance, but at all costs, there are costs. You can't expect to get ahead when you keep doing the same thing you've been doing. You have to make a change.

If money is what you're worried about, there are literally thousands of people with money that don't have the knowledge to execute on an idea. Many partnerships start from one person bringing the money and one person bringing the knowledge. Define what you want to do and learn everything about it. Know your market and know your business inside and out before you start. This will take some of the fear and unknown out of the equation. Be confident and find someone who can compliment your skill set to better achieve your highest goals.

Make step one getting your real estate license, learn your craft inside and out. Step two should be to save enough money to have a financial foundation while on your journey (having your license should be able to bring you plenty of extra money to do this). Step three should be to define your goals. Figure out exactly what you want real estate to do for you. This will help you decide where you want to invest and what type of real estate you should invest in to meet your goals fastest. Step four should be to network with local investors, agents, mortgage brokers and anyone you feel may add value for you on your journey. After networking and growing your circle of influence you need to build your team. Step five should be to find a lender, contractor, agent (if you didn't get your license) and property manager (if you are going to invest in rental properties). This team will help you get everything you want out of real estate. Step six should be to start finding deals, having already decided on what you're investing in and where you're investing, you need to research the area and asset class and start viewing properties. After finding a suitable investment property you're off to the races. Close that deal and do everything you can to keep growing your portfolio. After getting over the hump of your first deal things will just get easier.

It is now time to get out there and execute. You will never get anywhere without making that commitment to yourself to be successful and take the leap. After making that decision, your life will never be the same. Pull those dreams into your reality. Stop day dreaming and start living.

The most important thing is to make progress. Make steps each day that will get you closer to where you want to be. They don't have to be big steps, but they have to be forward moving. The single biggest demotivator is lack of progression. If you can't see progress, why would you keep moving forward? Celebrate the small wins every day. Set small goals and acknowledge yourself when you achieve them. This will propel you into the right direction.

You aren't like the rest. The average household in America holds $16,000 in credit card debt and 60% of us have less than $1,000 in the bank. Everybody is different, but you're reading this because you have a dream and vision for your life, to create lasting wealth for generations and rise above the rest. With financial freedom you have an opportunity to live life on your terms and truly be in the moment because you aren't dwelling on what your future finances will be like. You have safety and security in knowing your finances are taken care of for life.

Life is about doing what you want to do, when you want to do it. Real estate can create exactly this, a life that has no limits by time or money. A life, worth living.

I want to thank you for taking the time to read this book. You are on the right track.

I am an open book for you, please email me with any questions you have or help you

may need. Real estate is my passion and I strive to help and support everyone I can.

evergreenbook@yahoo.com

Made in the USA
Las Vegas, NV
23 November 2020

11297773R30097